MODERN NOVELISTS

General Editor: Norman Page

MODERN NOVELISTS

MODERN NOVELISTS

MALCOLM LOWRY

Tony Bareham

St. Martin's Press
New York

First published in the United States of America in 1989

Printed in Hong Kong

ISBN 0–312–02445–2

Library of Congress Cataloging-in-Publication Data
Bareham, Tony.
Malcolm Lowry/Tony Bareham.
    p. cm.—(Modern novelists)
Bibliography: p.
Includes index.
ISBN 0–312–02445–2: $35.00 (est.)
1. Lowry, Malcolm, 1909–1957 – Criticism and interpretation.
I. Title. II. Series.
PR6023.096Z567 1989
813′.54–dc19   88–23360
                                                           CIP

Contents

For Margaret

Author's Note

I have written quite extensively on Lowry in the past, though not recently. Hence this book enabled me to make a re-evaluation. In some cases this has involved changing my mind, particularly about the short stories. I can only hope that readers find it a more honest stance on my part to admit that I was probably wrong in the over-enthusiastic appraisal I made of some of the material in *Hear Us O Lord From Heaven Thy Dwelling Place* in a previous evaluation, than to cling for consistency's sake to opinions I no longer really feel.

My thanks are due to:
Rosemary Savage, who typed the final copy of my tortuous manuscript; Harry McNulty, whose office equipment I wore into the ground; Professor Norman Page, and the staff at Macmillan, for friendly and well-directed assistance; John McVeagh whose always perspicacious comments have been responsible for numerous improvements to my original ramble.

The book was written on study leave granted by the University of Ulster at Coleraine.

Acknowledgements

The author and publishers wish to thank the following who have kindly given permission for the use of copyright material:

The Athlone Press Ltd. and The University of Chicago Press for extracts from Richard K. Cross, *Malcolm Lowry: A Preface to his Fiction*, 1980; Gordon Bowker for extracts from *Malcolm Lowry Remembered*, BBC, Ariel Books, 1985; Jonathan Cape Ltd. and the Executors of the Malcolm Lowry Estate for extracts from Malcolm Lowry, *Ultramarine*, *Under the Volcano*, *Hear Us O Lord From Heaven Thy Dwelling Place*, *October Ferry to Gabriola* (ed. Margerie Bonner Lowry) and *Dark as The Grave Wherein My Friend is Laid* (eds. Douglas Day and Margerie Bonner Lowry); City Lights Books for Malcolm Lowry, 'After Publication of *Under the Volcano*' from *Selected Poems*, 1962; Oxford University Press for extracts from Douglas Day, *Malcolm Lowry: A Biography*, 1974; University of Nebraska Press for an extract from Gerald Noxon, 'Malcolm Lowry: 1930', *Prarie Schooner*, Winter 1963–4, pp. 317–8; Vision Press Ltd. for an extract from Anne Smith, ed. *The Art of Malcolm Lowry*, 1978.

Every effort has been made to trace all the copyright holders, but if any have been inadvertently overlooked the publishers will be pleased to make the necessary arrangement at the first opportunity.

General Editor's Preface

The death of the novel has often been announced, and part of the secret of its obstinate vitality must be its capacity for growth, adaptation, self-renewal and even self-transformation: like some vigorous organism in a speeded-up Darwinian ecosystem, it adapts itself quickly to a changing world. War and revolution, economic crisis and social change, radically new ideologies such as Marxism and Freudianism, have made this century unprecedented in human history in the speed and extent of change, but the novel has shown an extraordinary capacity to find new forms and techniques and to accommodate new ideas and conceptions of human nature and human experience, and even to take up new positions on the nature of fiction itself.

In the generations immediately preceding and following 1914, the novel underwent a radical redefinition of its nature and possibilities. The present series of monographs is devoted to the novelists who created the modern novel and to those who, in their turn, either continued and extended, or reacted against and rejected, the traditions established during that period of intense exploration and experiment. It includes a number of those who lived and wrote in the nineteenth century but whose innovative contribution to the art of fiction makes it impossible to ignore them in any account of the origins of the modern novel; it also includes the so-called 'modernists' and those who in the mid- and late twentieth century have emerged as outstanding practitioners of this genre. The scope is, inevitably, international; not only, in the migratory and exile-haunted world of our century, do writers refuse to heed national frontiers – 'English' literature lays claim to Conrad the Pole, Henry James the American, and Joyce the Irishman – but geniuses such as Flaubert, Dostoevsky and Kafka have had an influence on the fiction of many nations.

Each volume in the series is intended to provide an introduction to the fiction of the writer concerned, both for those approaching him or her for the first time and for those who are already familiar with some parts of the achievement in question and now wish to place it in the context of the total *oeuvre*. Although essential information relating to the writer's life and times is given, usually in an opening chapter, the approach is primarily critical and the emphasis is not upon 'background' or generalisations but upon close examination of important texts. Where an author is notably prolific, major texts have been selected for detailed attention but an attempt has also been made to convey, more summarily, a sense of the nature and quality of the author's work as a whole. Those who want to read further will find suggestions in the select bibliography included in each volume. Many novelists are, of course, not only novelists but also poets, essayists, biographers, dramatists, travel writers and so forth; many have practised shorter forms of fiction; and many have written letters or kept diaries that constitute a significant part of their literary output. A brief study cannot hope to deal with all these in detail, but where the shorter fiction and the non-fictional writings, public and private, have an important relationship to the novels, some space has been devoted to them.

NORMAN PAGE

Introduction

Few modern novelists present more vexatious problems than does Malcolm Lowry. There are plenty of sources for the facts of his life, but it takes very little investigation to make one aware that these sources conflict, often contradict each other, and that they lend themselves to radically differing interpretations.

This account of the novelist's life uses three principal sources – Douglas Day's *Malcolm Lowry*[1], purporting to be the official biography; Gordon Bowker's compilation of interviews and personal accounts, entitled *Malcolm Lowry Remembered*[2]; and the *Selected Letters*[3], edited by Lowry's second wife, together with Harvey Breit. Here, one might think, would be a corpus of reliable and consistent material provided from among the reminiscences of the novelist's friends and contemporaries, from his own correspondence, and from a scholar dedicated to providing an accurate Life of the writer.

The problems are soon manifest. Day is horribly inaccurate. He spells names wrong, confuses dates, and blurs continuity of outline. Reading the reminiscences collected by Bowker it quickly becomes clear that Lowry presented wildly differing facets of his personality to different friends and contacts. Several of these reminiscences, moreover, have occasion to be partial, self-defensive, or less than totally frank. Even the letters, carefully sifted through, are those of a man who was frequently evasive, over-optimistic in his promises, unstable. Thus, there is not a single consistently reliable witness upon whom we may call.

This seems to strike a negative note in an attempt at presenting a clear outline of Lowry's life and work. With Malcolm Lowry nothing *was* clear or simple. He regarded life as 'a forest of symbols'; the phrase is Baudelaire's, and Lowry used it often.

He had an abnormal sensitivity to the power of coincidence and accident. He was so introspectively self-critical that he frequently lost track of the essential difference between fact and subjective wish. And alcohol wrought extreme changes, schisms and contradictions in him. To take but one example: his warmth and charisma of character are testified by source after source. 'The very sight of that old bastard makes me happy for five days' was the involuntary testimony of one friend. Yet the same man who inspired this warm praise could stagger drunk into a neighbour's house, stare at his handicapped child and ask, 'what kind of man are you if this is the sort of kid you produce?' (Day, p.462).

What kind of man was this indeed, who presented such divergent aspects of character to the world? Beyond a certain point it is none of our business. There will always be discrepancies between the morality of the created artifact and the social persona of the creator. But Malcolm Lowry carries this problem to its extreme. More importantly, because he is so predominantly an author who draws upon himself to create his fiction, we are bound to take some account of the nature and causes of these schisms.

There is yet another major problem of which the reader or student must be aware when coming to Lowry for the first time. His published output up to the time of his death in 1957 comprised two novels – *Ultramarine* (1933), and *Under the Volcano* (1947) – a handful of short stories, and a few poems. Most of the stories comprise material later incorporated into or ultimately associated with the novels themselves. Since his death there have been two more novels – *Dark As The Grave Wherein My Friend Is Laid* (1969), and *October Ferry To Gabriola* (1971) – two collections of short stories and novellas, principally *Lunar Caustic*[4], and more poetry. But every one of these posthumous volumes has been the work of editors combing through Lowry's papers.

After Malcolm's death his second wife, Margerie, made it her life's work to conflate and to splice into shape the multiplicity of drafts, notes, alternative versions, through which he worked. There are plenty of critical voices which argue that the posthumous fictions can scarcely stand for judgement as the work of Malcolm Lowry alone. Worse still for anyone attempting a critical overview, grave doubt is often expressed about the quality of this posthumous work, regardless of purity of authorship. Yet in most quarters Lowry is recognised as the author of one of the masterpieces of twentieth-century fiction. He emerges as that most vexatious of critical problems – the 'one book' author.

The one book is, of course, *Under the Volcano*. Frequently reissued, filmed, prescribed on many university literature courses, it is a brilliant, compelling and innovative work of high art. But nothing else he did is deemed to come within touching distance of it. Lowry demonstrates neither the relentless development in power and technique which characterises the growth of an artist like Dickens, nor the ability to leap forward over his intermittent lapses which marks the career of Hardy.

Goodness knows, this is not because Lowry was an occasional writer. He never had a job; he never did anything but write, supported for a good deal of his life by subventions from his father. Writing seems to have been as much a compulsion as a vocation.

His work methods are described more fully at a later point in this study, but the sense of near pathological commitment with which Lowry approached the creative process must be made clear from the outset. Why did a man so devoted – and so privileged – publish so little?

Though born in England Lowry lived most of his creative life abroad; in Mexico, in Canada, and on forays to continental Europe from his New World base. *Under the Volcano* and *Dark as the Grave* have Mexican settings; *October Ferry* is located in British Columbia; the very early *Ultramarine* takes place on a voyage to the Far East; most of the major short stories have Canadian or Italian backdrops. From the very early 1940s Lowry was virtually an exile from the English literary world. Actually isolated from nearly all outside influences, the most palpable were always American rather than British. Do we then place him as 'Canadian', 'Commonwealth', 'American', or what? This study will regard him, despite geographical factors, as still centrally English. I have written elsewhere in defence of this stance.[5] But the 'Lowry industry' has its critical headquarters in the New World, and its judgements of the novelist may be slanted or vitiated by a desire to 'claim' Lowry for a particular school or style of American writing.

Mention of the Lowry critical 'industry' raises another general problem of which the new reader should be aware. *Under the Volcano* is a wonderfully rich and complex novel. It needs many readings and substantial erudition to grasp the deeper layers of meaning which run down through its texture. At its heart there is a passionate clarity of feeling, but there have been too many critics concerned only with esoteric corners of the book.

Thus the biography is contentious, the material of the fiction often opaque, the validity of the canon difficult to establish, and the critical field cluttered. Beyond these problems again lie the specific issues of style, presentation, methodology and genre which must engage the would-be student of Lowry's art, and with which this introduction to the novelist seeks to deal.

1

The Life and the Milieu

Clarence Malcolm Lowry was born in New Brighton, Cheshire, in the north-west of England, on 28 July 1909. He was the youngest of four brothers in a well-to-do upper-middle-class family. Malcolm's relationships with those at home were severely fraught, and his tendency in later years to select and mythologise what happened often conceals the violent and anti-social nature of his behaviour. It is clear that he was never easy to handle, and that he was a constant source of anxiety and financial strain. Arthur Osborne Lowry, a cotton-broker, supported his youngest son by means of a generous monthly allowance, first at Cambridge, then in 'Bohemian' London, and later in America, Mexico, and Canada.

It would be no concern how father and son got on together were it not for the fact that Lowry's attitude to authority in his novels is of prime importance and may be fairly surmised to owe much to the real-life father/son relationship.

The novelist, to an extreme degree, seemed to fear and yet to need figures of authority around him. He was paranoid about crossing international frontiers; customs and immigration officers inspired rank terror in Lowry, who saw them as all-powerful figures of authority. As we shall see, the Mexican immigration authorities did give him an awful time in 1946, but everyone who ever travelled with him bears witness to the abject and irrational state to which Lowry was reduced by even the notion of immigration officers. Nearly every one of the novels involves this notion of 'Authority'.

At eight years old Malcolm was sent to prep school – Caldicott, near Hitchin in Hertfordshire, just north of London – whence in 1923 he moved on to The Leys, a public school in Cambridge. Lowry's own stories about the traumas of his early years must be balanced against the account given by other people. The novelist

painted a picture of a miserable youth in which he was mal-
treated by a series of nannies, misunderstood by his parents,
and subjected to various brutal experiences. These are drawn
repeatedly into the texture of his fiction. According to his brother
Russell, many of them are examples of fiction making in their own
right.[6] What the commentators find hard to explain is *why* Lowry
wanted to tell these apparently exaggerated or untrue stories about
his treatment in adolescence. He claims, for instance, that he
suffered from eye trouble as a lad, and that this was cruelly
neglected until he suffered the threat of going blind. Russell is
able to prove that this is simply not true. *October Ferry* reveals
an attempt to turn this imaginary illness into the matter for
fiction.

Another famous canard concerns his prowess at golf. In later years
Lowry told friends that he had been an international schoolboy golf
champion. He was, in reality, a reasonably talented but by no means
exceptional golfer. He won his age class in a local competition,
and this earned him selection to a schoolboys' championship in
London. On his return home it emerged that Lowry had not taken
part. Ostensibly he had suffered from food poisoning; the truth
of the matter was that he had got completely drunk the night
before the competition and was incapable of participating. Yet,
years later, in a letter to his literary editor, Lowry boasted of
his success in this competition, and of the equally apocryphal
record-breaking scores he recorded at golf.[7] Such myth making is
common enough. With Lowry, however, it was out of all proportion,
and became inextricably bound up with his work methods as a
novelist. Myth, fantasy, self-exculpation all form obtrusive elements
in his stories. They can often lead Lowry's heroes into a kind of
intellectual dishonesty which is not an intentional part of the plot
structure. Gordon Bowker observes: ' . . . one of his finest fictional
contrivances, it sometimes seems, was his own life.' (op.cit. p.9).
Bowker continues thus:

> From the moment he embarked on a serious writing career,
> he centred all his imaginative effort around himself. He sought
> experience and then turned these experiences into fiction, with
> the result that his novels . . . are intensely autobiographical and
> his central characters are all Malcolm Lowry in one guise or
> another. (ibid.)

It is the consistent and radical nature of this selective self-scrutiny which validates investigation of Lowry's childhood and the myths he constructed around it. Lowry's poem 'Autopsy' points us in the same direction:

An autopsy on this childhood then reveals:
That he was flayed at seven, crucified at eleven.
And he was blind as well, and jeered at
For his blindness. Small wonder that the man
Is embittered and full of hate . . .
(*Canadian Literature*, 8; Spring 1961, p.23)

An autopsy on the actual childhood reveals nothing of the kind, but a tension between the imagined suffering and the very need to imagine it renders urgent and pertinent the artistic outcome of the fantasising.

For most of his adult life Lowry was a dipsomaniac. Why and when his inordinate drinking began are shrouded in doubt.[8] Again what concerns us is that, drawing upon (but for once transcending) personal experience, Lowry has given us Geoffrey Firmin, the dipsomaniac protagonist of *Under the Volcano*, a uniquely accurate, horrific and sympathetic account of the workings of a drink-affected personality.

At his public school Lowry projected an image of non-conformity in dress, in deportment, and in intellectual tastes. Anti-establishment journalism and a penchant for jazz music are what his contemporaries most remember about him. He collaborated in at least two published songs – thanks to a subvention from his father – and was a passionate performer upon the ukulele. References and analogies to jazz music and to musical form are frequent in his writing. Later, as we shall see, he 'found' German Expressionist cinema. This, too, comes to form a strand of both his material and his methodology.

The elder Lowry boys had all gone through The Leys and on to Cambridge. It seemed a reasonable assumption that Malcolm would follow them. But his level of academic commitment was mediocre – or at least idiosyncratically selective, and a bargain had to be struck. He would graciously agree to go up to Cambridge only if he could first be permitted to make a sea voyage to the Far East. Arthur Lowry had mercantile marine connections through his cotton-broking business, and it was duly arranged that Malcolm should ship out as deck hand on the Blue Funnel freighter *Pyrrhus*. The boat, the voyage, and the sea itself feature largely in his writings. *Ultramarine*, Lowry's first novel, grew directly out of the *Pyrrhus* trip; in much of the later fiction the sea is an agency which divides cultures and which wreaks character metamorphosis.

Lowry left Liverpool on the *Pyrrhus* on 15 May 1927. The regular sailors resented him as taking a job from a lad who might genuinely need it. Lowry bore this resentment for the entire duration of the voyage – which certainly disappointed any romantic aspirations he had nursed. The experience fed not only *Ultramarine*, but several short stories, and the psychological hinterland of Hugh, the second protagonist of *Under the Volcano*. This last is by far the most fruitful influence, for the picture of Hugh, macho, guitar-playing, song-writing revolutionary, is informed by wonderfully self-aware authorial humour. The episode is under the control of a creative *discipline*, utterly without self-pity. This is all too rare in Lowry's autobiographical flashbacks.

Several authorities date the heavy drinking as commencing at this time. Dana Hilliot, the hero of *Ultramarine*, is himself an inveterate boozer – even the regular ship's company find it matter for comment. It seems as though Dana drinks to stave off the temptation to indulge in dockside brothel sex. The boundaries between fact and fiction become indistinct here.

Lowry returned in September 1927, bringing with him the germ of a novel. Russell Lowry remembers this early form of *Ultramarine* as being a comparatively simple and straightforward narrative of actual events. The final work is anything but that; Russell seems to be describing an early example of a typical Lowry work process, whereby the simple narrative line is steadily overlaid and encrusted with levels of symbolism and descriptive parabolas, and where the handling of time becomes less and less consecutive and linear.

From that time onwards Lowry had no career aspiration except to be a writer. By the time he entered St Catharine's College, Cambridge, in 1929, he had begun to impose upon all those around him the notion that he was a budding genius already steeped in the mysteries of English prose. The reputation he seems to have enjoyed at Cambridge was totally unvindicated by the amount of published work he had achieved, but he had certainly begun a process of making valuable contacts. Among these was the American poet and novelist Conrad Aiken (1889–1973), who was to become and remain one of the strongest literary and personal influences on Lowry.

Having missed the 1927 date of entry for Cambridge, Lowry sought an academic mentor for the intervening year. He wrote to Aiken, who happened to be in England at the time, and who was only too glad to take under his wing the uncritically adulatory Lowry. *Ultramarine* is heavily indebted in style and presentation to Aiken – particularly to his novel *Blue Voyage* (1927), to whose title Lowry's own pays homage. One may doubt the value of either the literary or the social influences of Aiken upon Lowry; strictly he must have been the very last kind of mentor Lowry needed, but the strength of the influence is everywhere manifest.

For better or worse the influence of Aiken sent Lowry in the direction of a highly decorated style and of a constructional method which eschews simple linear exposition of narrative, and which seeks to layer and overlap the description of experience until a poeticised impressionism supervenes. The two early Lowry letters to Aiken which are preserved in *Selected Letters* suggest that there was a mawkish and uncritical adulation behind this imitation.

During the same pre-Cambridge period Lowry went to Bonn in Germany (late December 1928–early 1929). Aiken had gone back to America and a couple of months at a high-class language crammer's on the continent was deemed useful. Lowry seems to have acquired little in Bonn except a taste for the local wines and for German Expressionist cinema.

Returning from Bonn, Lowry found Aiken had gone back to America, and in the autumn of 1929 the long-suffering Arthur Lowry was induced to finance another trip, so that Malcolm could join Aiken. More and more the father surrogate revealed himself as the direct opposite of the real parent. Aiken was a heavy drinker and at this time was going through a series of unstable domestic relationships. He offered a lifestyle quite the opposite of that obtaining at home, and certainly more congenial.

As a writer Aiken had manufactured a strongly post-Joycean style, and his handling of time was more like that of an Expressionist cinema director than a Realist novelist. Aiken had also experimented with a kind of montage technique in which conversations, impressions, snippets of material from time present, are layered on to the past. This chimed in exactly with Lowry's appreciation of the cinema he had seen in Germany.

October 1929 saw Lowry entered at St Catharine's College, where his interest in the official syllabus seems to have been pretty sporadic. He caught the university in one of its brightest periods. Retrospect may still make one envious; it must have been exhilarating to be 'up' with William Empson, T.H. White, Jacob Bronowski, and Kathleen Raine.

Another Cambridge acquaintance was the journalist and critic, John Davenport. He has recalled the wildly unconventional but fascinating selection of reading which Lowry substituted for the official English course.[9] He read the Elizabethans with enthusiasm; later, *Dr Faustus* was to become important in the background to *Under the Volcano* – and his bookshelves indicated a more than average acquaintance with Joyce, Eliot, e. e. Cummings, Wallace Stevens, and Melville. Thomas Mann, Dante and William Faulkner were well represented. Perhaps most surprising of all, at a period when he was far from fashionable, Henry James seems to have been studied by Lowry in real depth. Virtually all of these masters have an influence upon Lowry's own style and literary attitudes.

University contemporaries also noted Lowry's interest in jazz. And one further literary influence emerged. Nordahl Grieg, a young Norwegian, had published in 1924 a novel, translated into English in 1927 as *The Ship Sails On*. It concerned in highly elaborated prose the first sea voyage of an impressionable young man, and it chimed in almost uncannily with the work Lowry was himself attempting in *Ultramarine*. Scandinavia fascinated Lowry. This may have enhanced the attractions of Grieg. Lowry claimed that his maternal grandfather had been a Norwegian sailing skipper who went down with his ship in the Far East under romantic circumstances. Russell Lowry is more than a little sniffy about the accuracy of this tale, but some process of mythopoeic transference avowedly inspired Lowry with a desire to create 'nordic' characters. One of the fictional personae he often adopts is named Sigbjørn Wilderness, and the characters in the short stories sport names like Astrid, Sigurd, Kristbjorg.

Grieg's real importance, beyond whatever influence he exerted in the still-developing *Ultramarine*, lay in a probable voyage that Lowry made to visit him in Norway, during one of his Cambridge long vacations. Some doubt exists about the date of this pilgrimage – or indeed as to whether the whole thing is another Lowry fabrication. On the whole the evidence suggests that at some time in the very early 1930s Lowry did slip away on a freighter heading, in ballast, to Archangel. He seems to have left the ship somewhere *en route* in order to make contact with Grieg.

The creative end product of this was the commencement of a new novel, to be called *In Ballast To The White Sea*. This was never finished, and the manuscript was burned in an accident. But in the early 1940s many letters discuss it among the work in progress.

In the summer of 1932 Lowry just managed to obtain third-class Honours in his English finals. A couple of chapters of the still-developing *Ultramarine* had been published in university magazines, and Lowry had impressed a lot of people, on pretty tenuous hard evidence, that he had in him the seeds of real talent. It was a question (presumably not least for the long-suffering father in Cheshire) of the use to which this raw talent might now be put. There is certainly no documentary evidence of Lowry's intent to do other than continue to live off his father. After graduating he went to the Aikens, now living in Rye, Sussex; and by the autumn he had moved on to London. In the meantime *Ultramarine* had been finished, polished, and sent off for consideration to Chatto & Windus.

In London Lowry was, ostensibly, living in a temperance hotel, and under the tutelage of Hugh Sykes Davies, who had taught him for a spell at Cambridge. Neither factor prevented Lowry from becoming involved with the city's Bohemian fringe. Louis MacNeice, for one, remained unimpressed by the rather noisy posturing which was part of Lowry's social façade; Dylan Thomas, however, became and remained a friend. The Australian poet Anna Wickham was another acquaintance from this period, as was the novelist Arthur Calder-Marshall, who has left graphic accounts of his friendship with Lowry.[10]

Indeed, for all his faults Lowry was able to charm, to hold, and to create loyalty in a wide range of people, although many were subjected to the volatile and sometimes dangerous outbursts caused by his drinking and his uncertain temper.

In September 1932 Chatto accepted *Ultramarine*. Throughout his life Lowry was subject to – or caused – accidents and coincidences, and *Ultramarine* was subject to one of these. The publisher's editor left the manuscript in his unlocked car for less than two minutes and when he returned, it was gone. Thus it had to be patched together a second time through the various drafts and fragments which had been preserved by friends. Or so, at least, runs the story! By now, however, Lowry sensed that Chatto had been less

than wholeheartedly enthusiastic in acceptance of the book, and it
was eventually Jonathan Cape who took the revamped *Ultramarine*
for publication in the summer of 1933.

Early in that year, and partly as an attempt to remove Malcolm
from the unsatisfactory lifestyle he adopted in London, the long-
suffering Arthur Lowry sent him to Paris to study at the Sorbonne,
under the tutelage of another mentor – this time the painter
Julian Trevelyan, a friend from Cambridge days. This venture
achieved little more of its ostensible purpose than the earlier
German trip. By April Lowry was ready to accompany the Aikens
on a visit to Spain.

They settled in Granada, where Lowry took once more to serious
and prolonged drinking bouts. That is, until June, when into his
life walked a young American, Jan Gabrial. Ex film starlet, now
writer, she was tramping her way across Europe. Lowry became
'like a mesmerised owl' in Conrad Aiken's phrase, but the impact
of Jan was strong enough to quell, temporarily, the drinking and
the consequent anti-social behaviour. Jan's departure simply led to
a worse outburst; relationships with the Aikens became strained,
and the Spanish trip was aborted.

There followed another of those recurrent Lowry coincidences. In
the October of 1933 he wandered into the Alhambra music hall in
London and ran directly into Jan Gabrial again. Since it was at the
Alhambra, the Moorish palace in the city of Granada in Spain, that
he had first met her this was quite as much as Lowry needed to be
convinced of the hand of destiny at work, and a serious relationship
developed, leading to marriage, in Paris, on 6 January 1934. Jan's
personal account of her marriage to Lowry can be read in Bowker's
book. But by July things seem to have been going wrong and Jan
left for America.[11]

By the late autumn of 1934 Lowry had followed her and attempts
were made at a fresh start. In 1935, through various upheavals, we
find Lowry at last working again – now on *In Ballast To The White Sea*.
But another downturn in the marriage meant that by the beginning
of 1936 the couple were living apart, and Lowry's life had reverted
to the kind of sleazy bohemianism which had characterised his
London period.

By June 1936 his physical and psychic condition had degenerated
so seriously that he was committed to – or entered voluntarily – the
Bellevue Hospital in New York. Here he spent a period (something

between ten days and three weeks) in the psychiatric ward. This is another of the episodes where dates are contentious. Accounts differ as to the length of the stay and as to whether Lowry was committed by his friends, or whether he entered voluntarily in order to gain experience for a novella. (The latter is his own version!) These hospital experiences are important mainly because they became the material for one of Lowry's most intense and sharply realised pieces of writing – the novella *Lunar Caustic*.

Late in 1936 the Lowrys headed west to Los Angeles. There is some suggestion that this was in quest of writing work for the film industry. Lowry always retained an interest in film script-writing, at various times working on *Moby Dick* and on a monumental version of *Tender is the Night*. But for the moment nothing came of plans for script-writing, and they decided to move on to Mexico where, *inter alia*, the cost of living was substantially lower.

Arriving in Acapulco on 2 November 1936, the Lowrys went first to Mexico City, then fairly quickly on to the town of Cuernavaca, about fifty miles south of the capital. These bare biographical facts do little to suggest the portentous meaning they came to assume for Lowry. November 2 is the Day of The Dead in Mexico, and it becomes the key date in *Under the Volcano*. Cuernavaca becomes – at least in part – the setting for the novel, and subsequent events in the town are worked into its plot, principally Jan's final abandoning of Malcolm. Mexico itself made an immediate and enormous impact. The process by which Lowry turned its geography into the iconography of his masterpiece is discussed later. But the atmosphere of the country, its people, its language and customs cannot be over-estimated. Nor, as we shall see, its politics.

Conrad Aiken afterwards claimed that when he came to visit the Lowrys in Cuernavaca in May 1937 he saw a draft of *Under the Volcano*, already completed. But Aiken's visit, and the one paid later in the year by the Calder-Marshalls, disrupted the mood of comparative sobriety and stability which had obtained since Lowry's arrival in Mexico. Jan became more and more desperate and pessimistic about the chances of curbing the alcoholic excesses, as well as about other aspects of marital relationships with Lowry. One account of this period can be found in Aiken's autobiography *Ushant* (1952), another in Jan's recollections recorded in Bowker pp. 113, et. seq.

In any event the short-lived marriage was now heading for

its final collapse. In December 1937 Jan returned to the States
leaving Lowry in Mexico. Over the following Christmas he collapsed
completely, both emotionally and physically, in the city of Oaxaca
during one of the most traumatic phases of his entire life. *Dark
as the Grave* describes this period. Several letters and poems add
balancing evidence. Despair was complete. It is this anguish of
a man abandoned which is transmuted into the tragic tones of
Geoffrey Firmin in *Under the Volcano*. Henceforward Lowry's love
of Mexico was always mixed with a terror and abomination of
its casual cruelty and injustice. He certainly spent a spell in
gaol over that Christmas; whether as a drunken derelict or on
suspicion of being a spy it is now difficult to discern. In *Under the
Volcano* the 'infernal town of Parián' is a conflation of Cuernavaca
and Oaxaca as he remembered them from this period. And *Dark
as the Grave* shows how the traumas repeated themselves – perhaps
were somehow *invited* to repeat themselves – on a return visit a few
years later.

Yet even during this dark night of the soul Lowry formed a
friendship which was itself to become a vitalising force in his
fiction. Whether in real life the Mexican comrade's name was Juan
Fernando Marquez, or Fernando Atonalzin is not clear. Biographers
offer alternative identifications. But the character of this strong,
charismatic Mexican appears in *Under the Volcano* as Juan Cerillo –
and as Dr Vigil; and in *Dark as the Grave* as Juan Fernando Martinez,
the 'friend' whom the author-figure is seeking. He appears yet again
in an essay called 'The Garden of Etla' which Lowry wrote for the
United Nations World in June 1950 (pp.45–7). He seems to have been
a courier for the Banco Ejidal which, in the late 1930s was attempting
to promulgate the democratic redistribution of agricultural wealth in
Mexico. For Lowry he became the archetype of masculine virility
and altruistic devotion to a liberal cause. Indeed it seems to have
been the encounter with this man that first motivated Lowry to an
interest in politics.

By April 1938 Lowry had dragged himself from the drunken
slough of Oaxaca to Acapulco, and by July he had left Mexico
for Los Angeles. Whether he was actually deported or whether his
father's importuning extracted him from the country is unclear. One
final desperate attempt seems to have been made to patch things up
with Jan, and when that failed the separation became irrevocable by
mid 1939.

In fact by this date Lowry had met Margerie Bonner, who was to become his second wife. No sooner had they met than Lowry's lawyer, acting on instructions from Britain, arranged for Lowry to be sent to Vancouver. Here he was, a man of thirty, with no fixed employment, no independent means of supporting himself, a broken marriage recently behind him, deported or forced to leave Mexico under acutely embarrassing circumstances, and showing no real signs of producing work which would justify the long years of support and subvention which his father had invested in him. Sporadic work was in progress on 'The Last Address' – an early version of *Lunar Caustic* – and on *Under the Volcano*, but Lowry seems to have been hustled north with such haste that both Margerie and the manuscripts were left behind. If the idea was to separate the two it failed because Margerie loyally threw up her job on the fringes of the film world and, in August 1939, went north to join Malcolm in Canada. And thus commenced the most complete and fulfilling relationship in Lowry's life. Even this was latterly torn by violent strife, but for many years Margerie encouraged, supported, and collaborated in Malcolm Lowry's life and his art.

In August 1940 the tide turned – as far as it ever did for Lowry. He discovered that, for a peppercorn rental, he could obtain possession of a tiny wooden cottage in a fishing community on the Burrard Inlet at Dollarton, about ten miles outside Vancouver. There were to be three of these 'shacks': the first rented from August 1940 to April 1941; the second bought and renovated April 1941 to June 1944; and the third, built by the Lowrys themselves and inhabited until August 1954, when they left Canada for the last time. 'Shack 2' was burned to the ground, with loss of almost the entirety of *In Ballast to the White Sea*, though Margerie did manage to salvage the current draft of *Under the Volcano*. But with all the accidents, threats of eviction, and the natural hazards of wintering over in an uninsulated two-room wooden dwelling, separated even from the nearest store and telephone by a hazardous journey through forest where mountain lions roamed, there can be no doubt that this place sustained and comforted Lowry as nothing else in his life had done. The descriptions of 'Eridanus' – his own name for the Dollarton locality – which are contained in his letters evince a real sense of peace and equilibrium for the main part. And in the lyrical novella 'The Forest Path to the Spring' he achieved his most

reposed work of art as he lightly fictionalised the daily routine and
the sights and sounds of his 'Northern Paradise'.

It was in this atmosphere, with a new and close companion
and with a congenial background, that he laboured to complete
Under the Volcano, and then to go on creating novels which he hoped
would accrete around it to comprise a master scheme of interrelated
works which he called 'The Voyage That Never Ends'. There were
eruptions and major setbacks – increasingly so in the early 1950s
– and however much the boy scout in Lowry was tickled by his
frontier life it must have been pretty hellish at times for Margerie.
But all that said, this was the period in which this self-tormented
and self-lacerating man came closest in his life to finding harmony
and equipoise.

One of the principal causes of ongoing disquiet was the series of
threats by the Vancouver City Fathers to remove the squatters from
Dollarton in order to 'improve' the area. The theme of a threatened
eviction is present in much of Lowry's writing post 1940, and though
it would be foolish to call him an ecologist or a proto-'green' writer,
his passionate and often lyrical pleas for the simple and unpolluted
world of 'Eridanus' can seem strangely prophetic. This new brush
with Authority also brought out all the old fears and phobias.

The Canadian years were interrupted by three principal forays into
the outside world. In November 1945 the Lowrys set off for Mexico.
By this time a fourth draft of *Under the Volcano* had been completed
and sent yet again to the publishers. It was the dominating factor
of life at this time.

The Mexican trip was motivated by the combination of the need
for a holiday, by Margerie's curiosity to see the haunted landscapes
evoked in the novel upon which she had been collaborating so closely
with her husband, and also by a desire to make new contact with
'Juan Martinez', the friend from Lowry's Oaxaca days. The story
of that trip is told, barely fictionalised, in *Dark as the Grave*.

During that trip, on 6 April 1946, Lowry finally heard that *Under
the Volcano* had been accepted by the publisher Jonathan Cape, but
only after earlier letters had called for further wholesale alterations.
The result of this had been a rather half-hearted suicide attempt by
Lowry, and, almost simultaneously, a letter written to Cape pleading
for the integrity of the novel as it stood. This letter is of fundamental
importance to any study of the novel. Chapter by chapter Lowry
defends his structure, his characterisation and his ideas in the book.

It is one of the most lucid and comprehensive critical documents of this century. That it was produced during a period of such personal anguish simply makes it the more remarkable.

Mexico caught up with Lowry again, however, and after a period of hair-raising problems with the immigration authorities the couple were deported on 4 May. The pleasure at having *Under the Volcano* placed at last with publishers both in Britain and America must have been considerably soured.

In November 1946 the Lowrys took a vacation in Haiti on the strength of the success with *Under the Volcano* and were in New York on 19 February 1947 for the novel's American publication day. November 7 1947 found them on board the SS *Diderot* bound, via Panama, for Europe. This trip which had the joint purpose of introducing Margerie to the Old World, and of chasing up problems with the various translations of *Under the Volcano* was by no means an unqualified success. Lowry's drinking got out of control once more – or at least was more obtrusively undisciplined – and both France and Italy proved less than paradisal. But a hoard of material accrued, which would eventually find its way into the short stories on which Lowry would be working in the ensuing years.

They returned to Canada in January 1949 and the last truly creative period of Lowry's life began as he settled back in at Dollarton. By 1953 things seemed to be going well enough for the American publishers Random House to offer Lowry a generous three-year contract for ongoing work. But his eccentric creative processes, the highly idiosyncratic methods of composition he adopted, and the increasingly esoteric and personal nature of his subject-matter never seemed to reach a conclusion that a publisher was likely to find viable. Lowry frequently promised completed drafts either of novels or collections of short stories, but the one ran into the other, and the publisher's eventual disenchantment was understandable. Over this period, for instance, the relentless progress of *October Ferry* first delighted and then exasperated Lowry, who seemed to be taken over by the material involved in this project which began as short story, turned into novella, and inflated itself into full-scale novel. Had he worked upon *October Ferry* alone this would have been commendable. Sadly, he seemed incapable of putting it into a properly disciplined slot among his total work in progress.

In January 1954 Random House felt obliged to withdraw their

contractual support for Lowry. Many commentators believe that
this construed rejection was the catalyst in the steady decline of
concentration and solid achievement which now set in.

On 11 August 1954 the Lowrys left Canada for the last time,
bound for New York, and then onwards to Italy. Years of inordinate
dependence on alcohol were now taking their toll on Malcolm both
physically and mentally. Periods of violence and irrationality grew
more frequent, and Margerie on occasions went in fear of her
life. Work on *October Ferry* was virtually in abeyance, and other
tasks, promised to Random House, were shelved *sine die*. Lowry
was in and out of hospital – and gaol – and no longer reliable
or stable. By June 1955 the couple were back in London where
further hospitalisation ensued; this pattern of sporadic work and
frequent collapse continued over the next two years.

At the end of January 1956 the Lowrys moved to their last
home, a cottage in the Sussex village of Ripe, and it was there,
on 26 June 1957 that Lowry's life came to an end, contentious
and ambiguous as so much else in his life had been. The previous
night there seems to have been a violent quarrel between Malcolm
and Margerie. She fled for refuge to the landlady next door, and
when she went to take Lowry a cup of tea the next morning he was
dead on the floor. The stories proliferated. In a sense it is of no
matter now whether he intended suicide – a substantial number of
Margerie's sleeping tablets were missing – or whether he took the
pills by drunken accident. Or whether he choked and asphyxiated
on the remnants of the supper he had consumed. It is with Lowry
the creator that we are concerned, and probably *this* Lowry was a
spent force long before the final events in Ripe.

This biographical sketch of Lowry has sought to underline certain
qualities and preoccupations of the man because they are relevant
to the artist in him, and to the works he created. The 'Authority'
theme, for instance, has been played upon copiously by some commentators. Certainly one should be aware of the repressive father
and the curiously remote mother in Lowry's background. Healthy
father/son relationships are rare in Lowry's novels. Geoffrey Firmin's
father had walked off into the Himalayas to seek Shangri-La, and
Ethan Llewellyn's father, when present, had 'beaten him over his
chilblains with a razor strop' – and he, too, is described as 'having
made a retreat' (*October Ferry*, pp.23 and 8 respectively). Amateur
analysts can and do have a field day with such material. There is

no doubting Lowry's terror of officialdom, nor the role it plays in his creative writing. This motif is closely tied to the fear of eviction from Dollarton. Perhaps this is part of a larger fear of rejection; it is certainly present, and of major thematic importance in every work Lowry wrote after he found his 'Northern Paradise'.

Less explicable is the subject of Lowry, magic, and coincidence. In several novels and stories he uses characters who claim to have occult powers; Geoffrey Firmin is a student of the Cabbala, Cosnahan's mother in 'Elephant and Colosseum' was a white witch, and Jacqueline's father in *October Ferry* claims supranormal powers. The subject fascinated Lowry himself. Whether his interest was stimulated by a brooding sense of destiny playing tricks on him, or whether he began to wish upon himself unlikely coincidences through his curiosity about the occult one cannot say. His own accounts of certain incidents do make one wonder whether a specially malicious fate was pursuing him. After his second shack caught fire, for instance, he went to stay in Ontario with Margerie's relatives, and was hounded by mysterious fires wherever he went. Likewise numbers, dates and recurrences of situation really did seem to bug his life. Was his neurotic awareness cause or effect of these phenomena? The point is that nearly all his characters evince similar hypersensitivity to fate and coincidence. The very early *Ultramarine* is the only major Lowry fiction not to be dominated by this motif.

This biographical sketch has suggested the growing dominance of alcohol. From Dana Hilliot onwards virtually every Lowry hero is a heavy drinker, to a greater or lesser degree threatened by his own alcohol dependence. While this may be because he could only ever write about himself, it needs to be said that, artistically, the drunken hero suits Lowry's style and method very well. His prose style is tangential, layered, abstruse and allusive. The alcoholic dislocations of thought suit this kind of writing. At least, in *Under the Volcano* we are persuaded that they do. Whatever the reasons, this novel represents one of the most successful reproductions in our literature of a drink-ruined, but noble, mind.

Yet another manifestation of the authorial persona in the fiction is the sense of *acedia* or pathological sloth from which the characters often suffer. Wilderness, in *Dark as the Grave*, is the extreme case of this. It seems to have been something from which Lowry himself suffered. Margerie tells how rejection of one particular draft of

Under the Volcano left him prostrate on his bed, unable to move for days at a time. So Geoffrey Firmin is unable to act or even to react creatively when Yvonne returns to him in *Under the Volcano*. This acedia is a trait readily associated with heavy drinking. Lowry's own life manifests a pattern of frenetic bursts of writing – when he was in full flow he would stand writing at his desk for fifteen hours at a stretch – alternating with long spells when nothing got done. The idle spells were always the drunken spells. Did he drink because he couldn't work, or did he not work because he couldn't after he had been drinking?

Thus the closeness between Lowry and his male characters is of cardinal importance in understanding his work. This also shows itself in the environments chosen for his novels. The earliest is a tramp steamer in the Far East; it equates to Lowry's own voyage in the *Pyrrhus*. *Under the Volcano* and *Dark as the Grave* are set in Mexico – following two authorial visits. *October Ferry* is set on the Pacific seaboard of British Columbia, where the author was then living and its geography echoes a coach and boat trip actually undertaken by Malcolm and Margerie.

At its best this relationship between fiction and biography gives the novels sharpness of focus. It also enables Lowry's idiosyncratic work methods to function potently. He was an inveterate note-taker and recorder of oddities which he had seen and heard. Though he was clumsy as a linguist he was fascinated by phrases, by public announcements, by poster hoardings, and by random snatches of overheard conversation. All these would be noted down to be later woven into the fabric of his fiction. *Under the Volcano* is a triumph of the pregnant assimilation of such material into the symbolism of the novel. In *October Ferry* Ethan Llewellyn is assaulted by a series of roadside advertisements flashing past the bus. These, in various ways, trigger responses related to all the anxieties, traumas, and shibboleths which are plaguing him. Where the assimilation of this material is incomplete – where the patterns of intention remain obscure because they are buried in purely personal, authorial, responses – the result is merely quirky. Lowry's use of such material certainly does not always serve him well but, through studying it, we can see another of the factors which underlie his creative process. Public notices, odd place names – both of which are wonderfully illuminating in *Under the Volcano* – will assimilate readily enough into a novel once its overall narrative intent and posture are assured. But more personal material, such as other peoples' letters, conversations, intimate reflections, need more subtle handling. They have to be layered in to the texture of the overall design. And this Lowry does not always achieve. Sometimes the experiences are still too raw to fit the fictional reworking required to make a distanced and dispassionate account; they are random and self-centred. Sometimes the personal experience may be too subterranean, so that the uninformed reader is left merely guessing at the artistic purpose. Sometimes the design itself is unsure.

Lowry was not normally a novelist of character. Long as it is, he always insisted that *Under the Volcano* didn't have *time* to describe character as well as all the other things he wanted the book to do! It has been suggested that all four principal figures in the novel are manifestations of Lowry himself. Most authors achieve narrative distance by inventing ancillary characters who exist outside the central figure, and who share and diversify the central experience from radically different points of view. It is a grave liability in Lowry that in most of his novels he showed no signs of this ability to create 'alternative' characters.

Lowry is said to have been singularly weak in creating female characters. Reconciliations or new understandings between man and woman in the final chapters of his novels have no psychological validity because the author's own experience of women is so narrow, and selfish, that he does not know how to contrive a credible *rapprochement*.

It has also been observed, if a little unkindly, that all the Lowry heroines are virtually the same: petite, vivacious, bright, darkly attractive; and terribly, terribly, long suffering. Lowry's heroes, apart from Geoffrey Firmin, are all married to a cliché. Yvonne, for all her culpability, forces us at moments to see events from her point of view. This is unique in Lowry's work.

His work methods, his literary beliefs and intentions, are also idiosyncratic. Bursts of ferociously sustained creative energy alternate with periods of utter lethargy. Lowry was a slow starter, and would stand at his desk sometimes for an hour or more, groaning to himself, addressing marginal prayers – very appositely – to St Jude, for assistance. Then, on a good day, the groans would gradually give way to sniffs, and to silence as the mood took hold. But towards the end of his life there were increasing periods when Lowry could not make the psychic effort to hold the pen. Then he would stand,

the calloused backs of his hands resting on the desk, and dictate
to Margerie. Since, even at the best of times, he relied upon her
for critical advice and creative assistance, this brings us back to
the problem of the integrity of his work, even before we reach the
posthumous novels which she spliced together from rough drafts.

Lowry was a compulsive reviser and redrafter. He never regarded
anything he had written as complete; it is recorded that Margerie
had to wrest from him the page proofs of *Under the Volcano* because
he was still radically dissatisfied even after ten years of rewriting,
and of final acceptance of the work. At all stages of composition
he would create differing versions of an episode, a conversation,
a single sentence. His meticulous and tortured compunction over
his prose has been likened to that of Flaubert. But the end product
very often entirely lacks Flaubert's sense of *finish* to his style. At
its worst it could lead to more and more obfuscating detail being
shoe-horned into an already tortuous passage. Lowry is capable of
producing great swirls of dislocated, non-sequential blocks of prose
with alternate subjects, and no grammatical logic. The inevitable
impression is of a man who had not obtained mastery at the most
basic level. Vague talk of 'impressionistic' methodology does not
exculpate these passages – some of which are further analysed in
my chapter on *October Ferry*.

Virtually everything Lowry wrote began as a short story, and
moved erratically through an intermediate stage when he called it
'novella', and then towards fully fledged novel. This underlines his
highly personalised sense of the dynamics of plot outline, and the
relationship between centre and peripheries in his work.

His plots embrace quests, undertaken through journeys. Dana
Hilliot is on a quest for recognition through his sea voyage. Lowry
is not even interested in recording what Hilliot will become if and
when he has found himself; *Ultramarine* scarcely touches upon what
its hero will be once he disembarks. *Under the Volcano* is much more
complex; Geoffrey Firmin should be on a quest for *rapprochement*
with his wife, but his real quest seems to be for the entrance to
Hell. The one day's space of plot-time is occupied with a series of
physical journeys, whose inner significance is that each carries Geoff
further from Yvonne and closer to Hell. *Dark as the Grave* repeats this
pattern. Wilderness and his wife go back to Mexico, where he had
written a novel six years earlier. The novelist is seeking to lay all
sorts of ghosts, through a quest to meet up with the 'good angel'

from his earlier traumatic period. The relationship between quest and journey is again a major influence on style and structure. *October Ferry* is a one-day novel in its surface time scheme – the day occupied by a journey down the coast of Victoria Island and out towards Gabriola Island on the ferry. The quest is to find a living space to replace the threatened haven near Vancouver. Eviction is, of course, a kind of displacement of the spirit, and the quest is for much more than merely a new roof over their heads. And during that one day's journey Ethan relives in retrospect most of the key episodes in his life through associative thought-streams triggered by events and signs along the road.

There is a strong body of critical opinion which believes the failure of Lowry's work outside *Under the Volcano* is inevitable precisely because of this combination of highly personal subject matter working through the methods here described. With this limited and introspective equipment was Lowry doomed? He might write one great book if he could gain distance from himself, but it was always likely that everything else would simply be about a man who wrote one great book and could not repeat it! This is certainly true of *Dark as the Grave*, but *October Ferry*, where the hero is *not* a novelist, will not yield to the same simplistic explanation of failure.

Another problem with Lowry's work methods involves his habit of engaging with numerous different projects simultaneously. It is not the mechanical problem of the early Dickens who simply took on more commissions than he could handle, and thus perforce was working on three books at once. Lowry did this voluntarily – even compulsively. The process of genesis for all his later novels shows an authorial tendency to swop from one to another, to have temporary favourites – usually not the work he was supposed to be engaged with! And because the ethos of all the books is so similar, he sometimes found it impossible to control the boundaries between one and another. He speaks in one letter of *October Ferry* 'gobbling up' material which should have belonged to *La Mordida* (in itself one of several long-term projects which he never finished).

Yet another problem is his growing insistence that all his fiction belonged to a masterplan, to one grand *oeuvre* called, significantly, 'The Voyage That Never Ends'. There are several attempts in letters to explain this design to his publisher and agent. None of them are readily comprehensible. The end product is a mountain of manuscript, at bewilderingly differing stages of completion, and often bearing as much ostensible relationship to project A as to B or C which are going forward at the same time.

We must also take account of the role played by Margerie. As far back as draft two of *Under the Volcano*, that is, in the very early 1940s, her hand can be discerned in Lowry's work. She has left on record that they collaborated by Malcolm passing to her a version of the work in hand for her radical appraisal, sometimes even for rewriting. Margerie was herself a minor novelist; such collaboration must have always been fraught with problems.

'Why do you write?' was, inevitably, a question Lowry was asked. After all, nobody except himself compelled him to contract horrifying varicose veins by standing fifteen hours at a time at his desk. Nobody subjected him to the frequent self-torture which composition seemed to bring on. The answer, at least once, was 'Out of despair. I am always despairing, then I always try to write. I write always except when I am too despairing' (Day, p.400). Arthur Calder-Marshall, friend and fellow practitioner puts it this way:

> I think it would be true to say . . . that he was a martyr to his genius, that he was a literary Antichrist, that he sacrificed the vision of heaven in order to reproduce the vision of hell as nobody had ever succeeded in doing – that particular alcoholic vision of hell. I think he knew that he was damning himself (Bowker, pp.156-7)

This, of course, serves precisely as a description of Geoffrey Firmin as well as of Malcolm Lowry. Calder-Marshall even believes that the traumatic Christmas in Oaxaca was self-imposed – deliberate exploration. Lowry claimed the same thing for the period in Bellevue Hospital.

Thus we have to cope with an author who threw off a plethora of fragmentary writing, who was drawn into a multiplicity of tasks simultaneously. Yet he is remembered by his fellow practitioners for his 'persistence' (Calder-Marshall); and for his 'discipline' (Aiken). Another close associate, the Canadian broadcaster and writer Gerald Noxon, records Lowry's great concern over technique. He was anxious not solely for self-expression, but to retain contact with established literary values; 'He seemed to know what he wanted to say . . . but he was terribly concerned with how he should say it' (Bowker, p.51). And Noxon avers that Lowry was at heart raditionalist. *Inter alia* the influences upon him have been cited as authors like Joyce and Kafka. But Noxon found him essentially still rooted in the nineteenth-century realist tradition. ' . . . he was unwilling to adopt the kind of personal stenography which made the works of . . . Joyce and Faulkner superficially difficult for the reader' (Bowker, ibid.). Though this comment applies specifically to the early Lowry it urges us not to ignore the surface narrative-line in *Under the Volcano*. It avowedly has depths, levels, layers. But it is primarily a *story* – a marvellously gripping story and the clever gymnastics of occult exegesis should not blind us to Noxon's description of Lowry. Yet we have to concede that he liked to 'decorate the page', as he once put it to Conrad Aiken, and the constant reworking of his manuscripts never helps to *clarify* pure narrative outline.

This leads to a consideration of the totality of the manifest influences on Lowry, and to weighing them against what we can discern of the innate quality of mind in the man. He was extraordinarily well read, and had a retentive memory. A friend testified that he was one of the few novelists who could make Dante and Faulkner seem 'of a piece'. *Under the Volcano* demonstrates an organic acquaintance with Marlowe, Mann, the Cabbala, Dostoevsky, Melville, Goethe, Kafka, Rimbaud, and Ouspensky. It is perhaps not surprising that an early publishers' reader's account of Lowry was that 'He will never, I think, do four-square circulating-library books' (Bowker, p.82).

The relationship between dialogue and description is always critical in Lowry. He is often praised for a fine ear for reported speech. In his best work this is very true. But on occasion he can produce direct speech which is cloth-eared, downright embarrassing. The conversations between Sigurd and Astrid in the short story 'The Bravest Boat' are an example of Lowry conversation at a low ebb. The recollected dialogues between Dana Hilliot and his girlfriend Janet are even worse. Yet when Geoffrey Firmin is in full flight we are spellbound by the witty and passionate parabolas of his speech. This ability with dramatic speech often manifests itself in soliloquy rather than dialogue, in fact. Perhaps it is appropriate that an author who could only re-create aspects of himself, and whose fictive personae are so often locked in interior monologue should have this gift. The passages of *Under the Volcano* where the Consul is talking inside himself, where there is no objective addressee, are often the most intense and moving – and also the most disturbingly funny. For it is of urgent importance to record that there is a rich strand of comedy running through his best work. Sometimes this is manifest in purely verbal response – for example, the scatological mistranslations of the menu in Chapter 11 of *Under the Volcano*; sometimes it is broad situation comedy – as in the encounter between Geoffrey Firmin and his neighbour, Quincey (*Under the Volcano*, Chapter 5). Puns, wicked twists of meaning, delicious understatements all play their part in the comic underlay to Lowry's tragedy. His melding of comedy and tragedy is part of his Elizabethan inheritance. Personal friends testify to the sly grin with which Lowry would 'try on' the most extreme statements or attitudes in public. In the various intervening stages between total sobriety and unconsciousness he was reckoned by many to be wonderful fun to drink with, and to listen to. The most successful Lowry heroes are always those who, at moments, can see the funny side of themselves.

Other aspects of the personality and the techniques of this tortured and vexatious novelist will emerge in a study of the individual works. Lowry is a conundrum and a contradiction. Beyond the biographical sketch and the tentative critical outlines drawn so far, it must be the novels themselves which provide any possible answers to the problems he presents.

2
Ultramarine

The creative processes which produced Lowry's first novel might serve as a model for all his later books. *Ultramarine* stemmed from an event in the author's own life, it underwent a substantial period of writing and redrafting, and it was always regarded by the author as unfinished – even after it had been published. The story itself seems to have begun in a shorter and simpler form than the one we now have, and was augmented by successive layers of material. This is true of *Under the Volcano*; and though they were never finished by Lowry, the same pattern was emerging for *Dark as the Grave* and *October Ferry*.

Since the redrafting of *Under the Volcano* itself was to take ten years, and since Margerie appeared on the scene quite early in that period to begin her work of collaboration, there is a case for saying that *Ultramarine* may be the only Lowry novel which is entirely his own; even with this book there are several close-to-surface sources – Aiken and Grieg, particularly.

In May 1927 Lowry boarded the SS *Pyrrhus* bound from Liverpool via the Suez Canal for Shanghai, Hong Kong, Yokohama, Singapore and Vladivostock. As with so much of Lowry's biography, there is contention over events at the departure. Apparently he arrived at the dockside in the family limousine, having arranged that the press should be waiting for an interview. Later, after this had backfired on him, Lowry implied that it had been arranged by his parents. Russell is in no doubt that Malcolm stage-managed the press appearance in order to obtain notice for his two recently published songs ('Rich boy as deckhand' announced the *London Evening News* of 14 May; 'No silk cushion youth for me, I want to see the world, and rub shoulders with some of its oddities, and get some experience of life before I go back to Cambridge University . . .') Bowker, p.350. Experience he certainly

got, but it was far short of his romantic aspirations. Employment i
the merchant navy was hard to obtain in the mid-1920s, and th
resentment felt by the rest of the crew at the young toff who ha
been forced upon them was entirely justified. Lowry was made t
feel exactly what he was – an incompetent outsider with influenc
at 'the office', who had done a needy lad out of a job. The docksid
high jinks with the press cannot have made things any easier.

There is plenty of testimony that Lowry grew up in every wa
during those months at sea. Physically he seems to have fille
out and developed. Emotionally he had to cope with the dislik
and contempt of his fellow sailors. *Ultramarine* is a novel abou
an adolescent growing up. It records a process akin to that whic
Lowry himself experienced. Russell Lowry is insistent that ther
was no notion of Malcolm going to sea *in order to* write a novel, so w
may assume that it was the *Pyrrhus* voyage which first directed Lowr
towards deploying his own emotional experiences as the subject o
fiction. One of the incidentally sad features of the book is that
seems to imply that its hero, Dana Hilliot, has genuinely learne
from his unhappy experiences. In real life Lowry himself did no
He learned how to posture as a macho jolly tar, and it seems to hav
been on this voyage that the lifelong heavy drinking really started

Some accounts make the voyage of the *Pyrrhus* sound endles
in fact, the ship was back in Liverpool by the end of Septembe
The *Liverpool Daily Echo*, 30 September 1927, carried the story o
the local schoolboy who, 'armed only with a guitar', had made th
intrepid foray to the Orient. Describing his life at sea as like tha
of 'a domestic servant on a treadmill in Hades', Lowry averred tha
there had been some compensations:

> '. . . I am extremely glad I took the trip. I went for "atmosphere
> and I got it. I have seen the world, and been paid for doing it.'
> Despite his fourteen-hour day the young seeker after inform
> ation found time to entertain the crew with his ukulele . . .
> (This) . . . helped in some way to solace him for some o
> the dirty work he had to do, such as painting the inside o
> a coal-bunker and chipping the paint off winches . . .

Interestingly, Gordon Bowker reproduces a letter of retrospectiv
reminiscence from one of the sailors with whom Lowry mad
this trip (Bowker, pp.33–4). From this it appears that he was a

unmitigatedly scruffy and incompetent deck hand who '. . . wanted very much to shine, but . . . just could not make it . . . P.S. (He) . . . *was* a silk-cushion youth, regardless of his desire to travel . . .' This rather deflationary truth about the trip should be stressed because of the use to which Lowry put it in creating the fable of *Ultramarine*. In the book the homeward voyage is transformed into something of a triumph of acceptance and comradeship. Dana Hilliot has genuinely learned something and changed for the better. In real life we may doubt if Lowry did.

Virtually every eye-witness corroborates the physical change wrought by those months at sea. Russell Lowry says 'He had "filled out" to an extraordinary extent on hard manual work and (compared with the swill provided at school) good food, so he was no longer a boy but the hairy, barrel-chested man of many subsequent pictures' (Smith, op.cit. p.19). But Ronald Hill, his erstwhile schoolfriend and musical collaborator was 'terrified' by him when Lowry went to visit him after the voyage was over. Lowry burst into Hill's rooms at The Leys, extremely drunk, scruffy, and noisy. And for several years afterwards this rolling roaring pastiche of the manly matelot was put on at will.

Ultramarine itself covertly suggests that the drinking was a cover-up, a counterattack against the ship's crew who would not accept him, and that it may also have been used to suppress the urge for the promiscuous sex life so readily available from a ship in Far Eastern ports. Other evidence points to Lowry's difficulties in adjusting to sexuality, and to his exaggerated fear of contracting syphilis. These are used to creative effect in *Under the Volcano* as subterranean factors in Geoffrey Firmin's complex life. *Ultramarine* lacks the maturity to contemplate or to assimilate this material dispassionately, but its very existence is significant.

Lowry's first novel was begun soon after he returned from his voyage. At this time he was living at home, and was still on good terms with his brother Russell, who remembers how developing fragments of the story were read aloud to him, and offered for criticism. Interestingly Russell remembers this first tentative draft as 'just a straightforward account of what happened' (Bowker, p.36). In the published version 'what happens' on a literal level is probably the least important aspect of the novel. We are implicitly witnessing a typical Lowry act of creativity. Each draft becomes more heavily poeticised and abstract; the introspective life of the hero grows at

the expense of the 'linear' plot, and more and more passages of
tangential description are layered in to the texture of the work
Virtually all the manuscript of *Ultramarine* is now lost or destroyed
but the process of creation is clear enough by implication, and i
entirely consistent with that which Lowry pursued for all his othe
books. Naturally, in later works – particularly *Under the Volcano* -
the layered-in material is less derivative, often more organicall
germane to the overall themes being discussed. Lowry himself late
came to feel that there was much in his first novel which was clos
to plagiarism. Even the title closely echoes Aiken's *Blue Voyage* c
1927, which was one of the seminal influences on the early Lowry
An unpublished letter stemming from the period of the genesis c
Ultramarine shows how close Lowry felt to Aiken:

> *Blue Voyage*, apart from its being the best nonsecular statemen
> of the plight of the creative artist with the courage to live i
> the modern world, has become part of my consciousness an
> I cannot conceive of any other way in which *Ultramarine* migl
> be written . . . Nevertheless, I have sat & read my blasted boo
> with increasing misery: with a misery of such intensity that
> believe myself sometimes to be dispossessed, a spectre of you
> own discarded ideas.[12]

Certainly Aiken's style encouraged Lowry to create substructure
around purely narrative surface in his work. Other principal ir
fluences on the young writer seem to have been Eugene O'Neill'
play *The Hairy Ape*, the poetry of T.S. Eliot, and, a little later or
Nordhal Grieg. The motif of the sea in other authors as diverse a
Rimbaud, Conrad, Melville and Jack London has been discerned b
commentators on Lowry's first novel. It is scarcely surprising tha
the stylistic texture of *Ultramarine* appears so restless and variable

By January 1930 a first full draft of the novel was probabl
extant, but a full year later this was still being altered and adde
to. Even by the Easter vacation of 1932 Lowry was ready to augmer
and polish, as the final version was completed under the aeg
of John Davenport. Then, as already described, the manuscrip
submitted to Chatto & Windus on 1 September 1932 was lost an
over the Christmas of that year a hasty rewriting was undertake
from whatever material had not been destroyed.

It is easy now, in retrospect, to make condescending judgement about Lowry's first novel. 'Derivative', 'experimental', 'imitative' were phrases used by the reviewers. Of what first novel might not these terms be employed? *Ultramarine* is palpably the work of a very young and impressionable man. But with all its uncertainties, lack of clarity, and failures to amalgamate stylistic influences into a unity, it is a brave book, with a clear sense of purpose. A 'straight' linear narrative, an overt fictionalisation of the *Pyrrhus* experiences, would have been easier to achieve, but this was precisely the kind of fiction Lowry did *not* want to write. The intellectual climate of the period incited his natural tendency towards complexity, and towards cerebral rather than physical development in the plotting. The climate created by Joyce and Eliot must have been impossible for an ambitious young Cambridge undergraduate to resist.

The later drafts of the book were written during his student days. Undergraduate writing is often 'showy'. And he was, peripherally at least, a part of the same undergraduate circle as the immensely witty and erudite William Empson. Everything would have been pushing him in the direction of complicating, psychologising, and poeticising the flakes of straightforward narrative in his first novel.

Nor is it an elaborate book merely for show. Lowry, for all the vagaries of his work methods – perhaps precisely *because* of them – was a serious craftsman. The problems of style and presentation exercised him acutely:

> For Malcolm it was necessary that his writing should have a perfectly wrought surface meaning, in the sense of the term established by Flaubert. A competent and thoroughly understandable narrative technique, however complex it might be in form, was a necessity . . . But while fulfilling all the conditions mentioned above, Malcolm insisted that his writing must be capable of carrying meaning at many different depths, on the many different levels of intellectual and emotional communication which he discerned so clearly in Melville, for instance. (*Prairie Schooner*: Winter 1963–4, pp.317–8)

It is thus that a Cambridge contemporary, Gerald Noxon, expressed the problem of the balance between the surface and the undercurrents in Lowry's chosen style of writing. The very extent of Lowry's eccentric reading may have hampered critical discrimination.

Finding one's niche among admired authorities as diverse as Bunyan, O'Neill, Poe and Dana – as well as all those already cited – cannot have been easy. We can scarcely be surprised if the finished texture of *Ultramarine* is patchy. Despite Lowry's perennial fear of being deemed a plagiarist, however, the identifications are honourably assimilated into the intellectual attempt he is making in the book to portray the psychic development of his hero. The attempt is the more brave given that the author's own mental development may have been anything but assured.

The diverse influences are by no means always successfully folded into the texture of the style, but *Ultramarine* is a brave and interesting first novel. It probes with some acuity at the psyche of an inexperienced and lonely young man, who, however gauchely and clumsily, is attempting to strike a rapport with his fellow men and with his own developing conscience.

Another liability of Lowry's work method must be reiterated here. He is not a novelist of character, in the conventional sense. 'He was incapable of inventing anything. He couldn't take a character . . . and elaborate it into a story. He could only take what happened to him or what he had seen, and embroider it . . .': such was fellow novelist Calder-Marshall's opinion.[13] Given this limitation and given Lowry's preoccupation with style, it is easy to see how emphatic a burden must be borne by the quality of the 'embroidery'. It seems to work best in *Under the Volcano* because there all the elements have an integral strength. The maturity and suffering of Geoffrey Firmin are ramified by the charisma of the strongly drawn settings, and by the layers of legitimate meaning – political, psychic, emotional – which the story throws up.

Often Lowry's handling of time within his novels exacerbates the problems. He once joked proudly to Aiken that he managed to make *nothing* happen in his novels. An inordinate burden is thrown upon style to carry plot. Few Lowry novels occupy more than a short period of consecutive present time. By offering four principal characters and by tracing their past interlinkages in time, as well as their present emotional state, Lowry avoids this feeling of thinness in *Under the Volcano*. Elsewhere he is always alarmingly at the mercy of the intellectual performance managed by his one isolated protagonist. In neither *Dark as the Grave* nor *October Ferry* is there any development in the psyche of the wife/companion figure who accompanies the central character.

In *Ultramarine* Hilliot is very much an outsider and a man alone. Lowry chooses to try and make us see how he develops intellectually across the space of only four days. The problems are considerable, and virtually force upon him the retrospective and introspective style he adopts. The 'story' is not told, day by day, from Liverpool out to the ship's destination, and then homeward again. It begins on a Thursday afternoon, about an hour before the *Oedipus Tyrannus* ties up at Tsjang-Tsjang. Six chapters later it has taken us only to her departure on the following Sunday. Yet in terms of 'subterranean' time we are transported not only back across the previous stages of the voyage, but beyond that into the early youth of Hilliot in Norway, and through the days of his courtship with his girl, Janet, in Liverpool and Oslo. Virtually as much of each chapter is occupied with time past as with time present.

The plot itself is disarmingly simple. The events of the stay in Tsjang-Tsjang are thinly spread, and have little intrinsic interest. On day two the galley mate, Norman, rescues a stranded pigeon from the ship's mast, much to the chagrin of Hilliot who wishes he had had the courage to undertake the act. On the Friday – day three – we follow Dana through the crushing routine of his daily chores on board ship, and the antagonism between himself and the cook, Andy, is emphasised. Only on the following evening does he venture ashore, intending to have his first sexual experience in the brothels on the dockside. He is fearful of betraying Janet, but under urgent pressure, he feels, to prove his manhood to the rest of the crew – Andy in particular. A drunken evening becomes more and more confused, until Hilliot is incapable of sex at the critical moment. When he finally sobers up enough to return to the brothel he finds his tart has been usurped – by Andy himself!

In Chapter 4, at lunchtime the next day, Dana finally explodes into an open quarrel with the cook, while in the next chapter, which takes place around 4 p.m. on the same Sunday, Norman's pigeon is lost overboard and Hilliot makes a half-hearted offer to risk the sharks in the harbour and save it. The offer is seen as a token of Hilliot's manhood, steels him to a final *éclaircissement* with Andy, and creates an understanding between them.

Chapter 6 takes place later that night, as they steam away from harbour, and implies that Hilliot is now accepted among the sailors; especially when, right at the end of the book, he is 'promoted' to

joining the firemen in the engine room, and relieved of his menial
tasks as deck boy.

By divorcing plot from meaning in this arbitrary manner it is
possible to underline the differences between Lowry's intention
and those of the other writers about the sea with whom he claimed
affinity. After all, over half the plot of *Ultramarine* takes place in
harbour and not at sea at all. The plot structure is merely an
excuse for the real purpose of the novel, which is to investigate
the idiosyncratic sensitivity of a young man undergoing a crisis
of identity and self-discovery. Most of the scanty incidents in
the story did happen to Lowry, and are transferred to Dana.
It is important to realise that the processes of self-scrutiny and
adjustment are common to both author and hero. Lowry himself had hypersensitive fears about contracting syphilis; so does
Hilliot. There was, on Lowry's voyage, a tame pigeon which got
lost overboard. The general discomforts of a deck hand's life are
accurately recorded from reality. What matters is the imaginative
redeployment of these trivial realities into a pattern which carries
a valid and larger meaning.

The true theme of *Ultramarine*, then, is a young man's quest
to prove himself a man among men, and yet to retain contact
with an alternative 'feminine' world where love and finer feelings
can be legitimately expressed – a search for the integrated identity
which Lowry himself never fully achieved. This also involves Hilliot
in asking radical questions about the *artist vis-à-vis* the *man* in himself.
Throughout the novel the highly self-conscious thought-streams of
Hilliot present him as archetypically the artist seeking to arrange
and balance the random phenomena of observed reality. He tries to
talk things into place as he seeks a repose between the polarities of
male/sexual and female/drink orientated worlds. This embodies an
intelligent if instinctual stab at self-awareness and self-analysis on
Lowry's part. It is partial, sometimes gauche, and incomplete:

> Dana has no idea what the basis of this new selfhood will
> be. But he is surely correct in thinking that the 'I' he wishes
> to become can be attained only by an outward reach of love,
> by acting in a way that transforms himself and his culture
> at the same time. It is, of course, an extraordinarily difficult
> project, and one that has scarcely begun as *Ultramarine* ends. In
> his first novel Lowry merely broaches the question of identity

to which he returns in all his subsequent writings. (Cross, op.cit., p.10)

The novel is about discerning the means of establishing a balance in life. The correlatives of choice are Andy, the apparently manly, assured, popular cook; and Janet, the gentle, virginal, diffident girlfriend. It is surprising how many levels of implication Lowry can raise through his contrastive deployment of these two.

The principal means of effecting the contrast is by subtle inter-cutting between time past and time present. Chapter 1 soon estab-lishes this, describing the past and present of Dana's mental state when the voyage commences. We are able to extrapolate for our-selves the further development by the time it ends:

. . . there was precious little meaning left now in this life which so surprisingly had opened out before him. Nor could he see why he had ever been fool enough to set this seal upon such a wild self-dedication . . . Not, at any rate, to himself, a man who believed himself to live in inverted, or introverted, commas; to a man who saw the whole damned business in a kind of benign stupor. (p.18)

False and assumed literary values (inverted or introverted commas) must yield to a freer interpretation of life. The *conscious* dedication of the commitment to the sea voyage is inadequate in itself. What the book strives to show is that this initial viewpoint lacks experience. A new wisdom will dawn by the time of the voyage home. It is through understanding himself in relationship to Andy that Dana is directed towards a new experience and understanding of larger issues.

He recalls how he had picked out the ship's cook right at the start of the voyage, as the crewman with whom he wished a particular friendship. Perhaps Lowry's ambivalent feelings about Authority – especially paternal authority – are implicit in this. Then his thoughts sweep across time and space to Janet, who has hitherto been the emotional centre of his life. The themes of friendship, acceptance, and validity of relationship are made inter-dependent. Janet and Andy represent polar opposites of Authority, though the over-simple equation suggests that Authority equals companionship.

For most of the novel Hilliot struggles to assimilate and reconcile them. We are led to believe that it must be *either* Janet or Andy:

either the newly experienced world of masculine independence, or
the closeted and known world of female-dominated domesticity
Both are choices of *present* condition; the *future* is still to be deduced
from them. It is a sign of instinctual wisdom in Lowry that he is
able to carry these potentially jejune clichés to a conclusion where
they have validity.

Hilliot's abortive attempts to 'prove' himself on board ship
are clumsy if misguided (indeed ludicrous) gestures towards
experiencing Andy's world – or what he thinks Andy's world
is. Very near the end, after he has broken through the cook's
hostility, it is revealed that what he has been seeking is a chimera
Dana explains this revelation in a letter to Janet:

> I have made it up with Andy! Early this evening, over a bottle of
> whisky, I told him of my love for you – and what do you think he
> replied? He replied that this love business fair used to make him
> tremble at the knees! But that he'd had it all knocked out of him
> now . . . (p.170)

Andy expands upon the disappointed and tawdry life he experiences
during his shore leaves. After a couple of days he is drinking too
much, sleeping around, simply waiting for his next trip abroad
The apparently charismatic male self-containment Dana thinks
Andy represents does not exist. It is an emotional and intellectual
treadmill. Dana concludes:

> So now I have a perfectly clear vision of myself: I find myself
> as a creature of luck: I have something Andy, really, except
> perhaps, as a fantasy in youth, has never thought of; a promontory
> from which I incredibly look down on the insignificant race of
> womanisers. (*idem.*)

This, tragically, is light-years away from the final vision of hell
which Geoffrey Firmin is to be granted. The essential difference
between the heroes of Lowry's two first novels is that while the one
– Hilliot – is still learning, and is leaning towards a hopeful and
integrated view of the world, the other – Firmin – already *knows*
and all his knowledge is infernal and destructive.

But at this moment, in 1933, Lowry/Hilliot can feel that he has
outgrown Andy, learning to replace him with something better. It is

curious that, after his first novel, which may be his most optimistic, the next most hopeful Lowry book is his last – *October Ferry*.

Dana exclaims, 'I have surrounded Andy's position instead of being baffled and hurt by it.' Furthermore, he can now see how Janet has a place in the new equation he must make out of his life. Earlier, in moods of frustration, he had railed at her, declared his detestation for her determined virginity. But now he sees that

> . . . yourself acting as an inhibiting factor are at the same time a sublimatory factor . . . being in love with you I have the universal experience of sublimated all-embracing love for mankind. (p.170)

This awareness spills over onto his feelings as creative artist, takes him beyond introspective posturing:

> My writing? You or any woman can do that for me. I don't know a damn thing yet. But one day I shall find a land corrupted and depressed beyond all knowledge, where the children are starving for lack of milk, a land unhappy, although unenlightened, and cry, 'I shall stay here until I have made this place good' . . . and though I admit all this is ridiculous, this is the only way to make our love our own in the eyes of God, the only manner in which I may learn to pity others without pitying myself . . . (p.171–2, *passim*)

In one way we have heard all this before; it is the evocation of the growing-up pains of each one of us. Lowry's attempt to give shape to these commonplaces by the *form* of his work validates the feelings and it is tragic to sense the resonances echoing forward to *Under the Volcano*. Again one senses how entirely opposite Hilliot and Firmin are. While the young protagonist of the first novel prepares to go out, as an integrated man, to do battle, we are aware that his greatest creation from the later work has abdicated all sense of hope or social mission. Lowry/Firmin found that 'land corrupted and depressed' in Mexico. But the discovery avails nothing. Far from 'staying until (he) has made this place good' he is in a last desperate retreat from it. It is in Ethan Llewelyn, the last Lowry novel-persona, that we again discern a genuine yearning to use his life in the service of others.

Such, then, is the broad outline of the moral intention of

Ultramarine. Callow, inexperienced, tentative, it is yet a real attempt
to define and grapple with the problem of achieving true adulthood.
Certain questions and certain critical reservations remain. First and
most obviously, the figure of Andy is invested with a cardinal
responsibility in the novel's strategy. On the surface the problem is
simply, that Andy is not worth the adulation which Dana heaps upon
him. He never says or does anything to warrant the feelings of hero
worship he inspires in Hilliot. He is insignificant and undynamic,
chinless, unintelligent, unfaithful, and tawdry. It may take more
than one reading to realise that this is precisely the point. The
tragi-comedy of Hilliot's attitude to Andy prior to their quarrel
depends upon us seeing further than Dana can. But the narrative
stance is so Hilliot-oriented that we have to learn to discern for
ourselves, exactly as Dana does. Then suddenly the false heroics of
shinning up masts and diving into shark-infested harbours fall into
place. They have a subterranean comic ambience. They epitomise
misconception of the true seriousness of life. We shall find in *Under
the Volcano* that it is Hugh, the younger half-brother, who resembles
Hilliot more than Geoffrey himself. Hugh is an 'indoor Marxman', a
middle-class revolutionary, dreaming of romantic gestures in Spain
and China, fighting for the liberals against the fascists. He wears
macho cowboy costume, and makes a spectacle of himself at the bull-
throwing. Nothing much lies behind his gestures, though. Hugh has
never really grown up. But he is now in his thirties. Hilliot, at twenty,
exhibits more potential for growth.

Thus, if on the first reading Andy seems to be a problem as far
as the ideological 'weight' of the book is concerned, that problem
disappears once the overall scheme of its structure is apprehended.
It is noticeable that as long as Dana fails to understand Andy he
misreports and misrepresents him. Once he has 'surrounded Andy's
position' the descriptions of the cook change subtly. We suddenly see
not an ugly, tawdry bully, inhibited by the manifestations of his own
inverted snobbery, but a rather sad and very ordinary little man, a
perfectly explicable amalgam of normal likes and dislikes; indeed, a
man with a perfectly valid point of view, however limited; a literary
'hero' akin to Prufrock or Mr Polly, perhaps.

A much greater problem exists with Janet, the opposing force
in Hilliot's background. She is at the disadvantage that we never
actually meet her in the narrative time-present of the novel. She
exists entirely in Dana's retrospections. The creative effort of making

convincing – or worthwhile – a rather twee virginal middle-class schoolgirl is quite beyond Lowry. He was seldom able to make his female characters have an individual life, and Janet is manifestly the weakest of all of them. Probably at the time of writing the book Lowry was still himself a virgin, with virtually no experience of the distinctive realities of female nature and sexuality.

Douglas Day avers that Lowry's first love affair occurred on the 1929 visit to Aiken in America. Its subject is identified as Dolly Lewis. Lowry wrote her a quite extraordinary love letter from on board ship, on his way back to England at the end of that trip:

> I would love you the same if you had one ear, or one eye: if you
> were bald or dumb: if you had syphilis, I would be the same . . .
> (Day, p.109)

But it was a very brief encounter, apparently entirely innocent. They spent their time mainly in rambling about the New England countryside and foreshore. At the time he wrote *Ultramarine* there had been nothing more intense in his experience than this schoolboy passion. If the Dolly-idyll is the basis of Janet in the novel, the inadequacy of her as a character is explained. Never for one moment does she achieve a level where we can consider her as a serious alternative to the tarnished, but adult, world of the ship's crew.

Ultramarine is Lowry's most sociable book. Elsewhere he usually deals with the introverted isolation inside the mind of one man who is cut off from group activities around him. In *Under the Volcano* Geoffrey keeps running away from doing things with other people; even when he arranges for them all to go to the bull-throwing in Tomalín, he isolates himself from Hugh and Yvonne. He spends most of their communal meal in the lavatory and finally runs from their company to find 'hell'. Neither Wilderness nor Llewelyn relate to groups of people; they lug around with them the mother/companion surrogates to whom they are married, and talk to them occasionally, seldom to anyone else. But one can feel moments of real shared companionship in *Ultramarine*. The German wireless operator with whom Hilliot strikes up a relationship is an illustration of this. And in the last chapter, what Dana has achieved is an entrée into the world of good humoured chaff and ragging which

marks the members of the forecastle. He is encouraged to entertain
them with his ukulele.

This merely underlines and exacerbates the problem represented
by Janet as a moral and spiritual correlative in the book. There
are passages in *Ultramarine* – always associated with her – where
the writing becomes painfully mawkish and immature. When it is
focused upon Janet, the book has no centre of experience to underpin
its imaginative quality. This side of *Ultramarine* needs to manifest
tenderness, and it is a quality Lowry knows nothing about. Thinking
about the child they may have if he returns home chaste, and of
their domestic rapport in time to come, Dana rhapsodises thus:

> Proud parents, Janet, proud parents when we give him, as a
> reward for good conduct, his digestive biscuit . . . His pyjamas,
> blue with a white stripe. Sliding into slumber down the smooth
> snow of sheets. The soft white curtains bellying inward, blown
> softly by the summer breeze. The clock on the wall saying – what?
> Tick tock? Tock tick? Time? Peace? Peace, peace, peace, says the
> clock. The child sleeps, we draw back the curtains, and look out
> over the drowsy garden; from the fields comes the murmur of
> falling dew . . . (pp. 65–6)

Presumably this was always going to be the most difficult part of
the book to make persuasive. It required Lowry to draw on a kind
of imagination he did not possess. It manifestly fails, both in taste
and style. One suspects, in fact, that style may here be under the
requirement to do all the work that imagination has failed to achieve.
Not even the escape clause, that it may be mawkish *on purpose* (since
Dana does not understand Janet) exonerates this excerpt.

In general, and as one might expect from a self-conscious young
craftsman at work upon his first major piece of fiction, style is a
problem throughout *Ultramarine*. 'He could not borrow or adopt a
style. He had to create one of his own to fulfil his own needs, and it
had to be forged out of the extraordinarily complex alloys which were
constantly being produced in . . . the furnace of his mind.'[14] Thus
Gerald Noxon recalls Lowry's insistence upon the quality and kind
of expression through which his narrow and introspective fictional
vision must needs be filtered.

In *Ultramarine* perhaps the alloys are still mixed with impurities,
maybe the furnace is not at a high enough temperature. The novel's

style is, in any event, patchy. The problem is exacerbated by the fact that there is no sense of steadily unfolding narrative line to hold the disparate experiments together.

It is easy to pick out the kinds of writing being attempted, often to attribute them to a specific source. The Expressionist cinema Lowry had assimilated in Germany may also be an influence upon the way he handles description. *Ultramarine* opens with a flashback of the crew signing on; this is recorded through direct speech, with no external interposition from an omniscient narrator. But Chapter 1 is later conducted through such a narrator. The book plays with narratorial stance throughout its six chapters. This can be suggestive and atmospheric, but can become wayward as several conversations are layered onto each other. The last chapter has more of this kind of writing, as we are shown how Dana is now accepted in the fore-castle. Here the device not only records the random and easygoing aimlessness of the close little male society. Its stylistic echoes of the manner of Chapter 1 make the contrast much more pointed. Instead of the terse and desiccated speech patterns of the individual seamen signing on, we are given the feel of their instinctual camaraderie, now homeward bound. There are eight pages of this. Then Lowry shifts his narrative mode. Dana opens and reads his one and only letter from Janet. Earlier he has been unable to bring himself to do this, but the new self-confidence of having been accepted by the crew gives him fresh animus. It provides a ready opportunity for a style shift in mid-chapter.

We again face the Janet problem. Her letter is a change from the rough, interlaced, male conversation which precedes it. But its naive and gushy tone seriously exposes her ingenuousness. Are we meant to see her as slightly feebleminded, or is this as near as Lowry can get to the way he imagines a loving and dependent young girl would write?

> I loved our talk our last Sunday evening just before you went home, because you were so manly, and you put things so simply and without making excuse for them, and I understood and felt proud of you. Please always tell me things in that way. I shall always understand if you do! (pp. 168–9)

It is this vapid gush which sparks Dana's imaginary reply, including the discussion of Andy already cited. It brings Janet and Andy as

close together as the novel ever allows them. But the final impression
is of a brave and meaningful experiment with style which has not
succeeded. Even allowing that *Under the Volcano* comes fifteen years
later, the difference in the quality of style between the two novels
is enormous.

The last chapter of *Ultramarine* also contains other experiments
with style which Lowry was trying out. Several times in the book
the narrative is set in parentheses of substantial length – pp. 62–3;
65–6; 68–70, for instance. These usually signpost the innermost
and most abstruse levels of Hilliot's consciousness. Their style has
a special fluidity. They often employ a particularly florid poetic
expressiveness:

> (Oh Lord God, look down on your unworthy and unwashed
> servant, Hilliot, the seaman, the Liverpool-Norwegian, whose
> knees knock together at thunder, whose filthy hands tremble
> always in impotent prayer; Oh Thou who createst my eyes from
> the green mantle of the standing pool, who createst everything,
> the weak and the strong, the tender and the cruel, the just and the
> unjust, pity his small impulses of lust, and see that little beauty
> in his life, which so soon shall be among the green undertow of
> the tides; and as he stands alone, naked, weaponless, deliver him
> from his bondage and bring him out of the darkness and the grief
> and the pain into sunlight.) (pp. 72–3)

This example represents Dana's mixture of terror, and resolution at
the moment when he decides he will risk the syphilis-ridden brothels
of Tsjang-Tsjang. These parenthetical episodes present alternative
thought-streams to the surface ordinarinesses of the crew's chatter.
They are the passages where style is most likely to become excessive.
The following, for instance, manifests an over-excitement with recent
reading of 'Prufrock' and 'The Wasteland', yet it is attempting
to give dramatic validity to the dislocated thoughts of Hilliot as
sense impressions flash by him on his drunken progress along
the quayside:

> Inside the church within the shadowy choir dim burn the lamps
> like lights on vaporous seas. Drowsed are the voices of droned
> litanies. Blurred as in dreams the voice of priest and friar. Cold
> hath numbed sense to slumber here!

No–no–no, said a train empty, the conductor talking to the driver from behind, leaning over his shoulder . . . (p.117)

A few lines later the stream of thought carries us into the patterns of rhythmic Greek verse which have interspersed Dana's reveries in earlier chapters. These, perhaps, link us back to Hilliot the public schoolboy out of place among the ordinary seamen of the ironically named *Oedipus Tyrannus*. And in that last chapter the stuffy classical verse is replaced by snatches of racy sea shanty:

> *And Jack went aloft for to hand the top-ga't sail.*
> *A spray washed him off and we ne'er saw him no more.*
> *But grieving's a folly,*
> *Come, let us be jolly,*
> *If we've troubles at sea, boys, we've pleasures ashore.* (p.163)

The insouciance of this ballad contrasts most markedly with what surrounds it, yet its cheerfully celebratory timbre now suits Hilliot's mood. Switches of rhythm like these between verse and prose are a feature of Lowry's work. In *Under the Volcano* they will be less obtrusive and contrived, will spring with more integrity from the narrative line itself. But even the more gauche experiments with rhythm, and the very appearance on the page of the prose itself in *Ultramarine*, show a deep commitment to style as meaning, and indicate an author bravely willing to take risks.

Lowry also shifts the narrative stance of his story to create variety and tension: Chapter 1 mixes flashes between direct dramatic dialogue and third-person omniscient narrator; Chapter 4 cross-cuts between present-tense conversation as overheard by Hilliot eavesdropping, and meditation upon that conversation which he imagines in the form of a letter he is composing to Janet. The range of stylistic tricks employed is, and is meant to be, disturbing and bewildering.

Some of this is manifestly an attempt to experiment with juxtaposed methods of story-telling and message-conveying. We cannot be quite certain that some of it is more than authorial hesitancy or even the effects of rewriting away from lost manuscripts. Lowry deserves credit, on balance, for attempting ways of pulling Hilliot's persona apart, showing how differing focuses of tension reveal different aspects of the character through alternative narrative stances. The Hilliot about whom the other sailors speak is a scruffy, inept, insignificant boy. But he has to coexist in this impressionistic novel alongside a young man with real sensitivity, who is painfully trying to find a balance and equipoise as he grows up rapidly. The narrative styles sketch out these alternative views.

For all its manifest faults *Ultramarine* is a brave attempt by Lowry to find a style and a subject. It may be true that he could not invent, that all his heroes are 'the abominable author' in thin disguise. Yet in this book he is wrestling to strike a balance between subjective identification with the neurotic and hypersensitive side of Hilliot, and a wry capacity to laugh at his protagonist. The processes by which Hilliot is allowed to find a point of accord with himself and with the rest of the crew justify themselves, and provide a springboard from which greater things can emerge in *Under the Volcano*.

3

Under the Volcano

Under the Volcano is Lowry's one undisputed masterpiece. A work of compassion, wit and tragic dignity, it invites comparison with the greatest novels of the century. It is not an easy book to come to terms with; its texture is enormously complex and dense. Levels and layers of meaning are thickly encrusted onto its narrative line. It creates its own poetical rhythm, and calls for many readings before it yields up its overlapping strands of associative meaning. It also has that rare capacity, granted only to the greatest works of art, that it manages to be at once marvellously immediate and circumstantial and yet, without forcing, it also achieves universality.

Like all Lowry's fiction, the events it describes are closely associated with episodes in the author's own life, but it embodies some of his most imaginative and suprabiographical writing too. In *Under the Volcano* Lowry transcends his own traumas and turns them into tragedy of a deeply moving nature. Moreover, in the great tradition of English tragedy, the work embodies some integrally related comedy of the highest order. It also demonstrates his adventurous virtuoso style at its most germane and well integrated.

The publisher's reader at Jonathan Cape who reported on *Under the Volcano* commented on its 'local colour, heaped on in shovelfuls'. Lowry rather deprecated this backhanded praise; most readers find the Mexican settings haunting, vivid, and convincing. Lowry's love–hate relationship with Mexico is here channelled into fine observation of the squalor and corruption, but equally into the haunting beauty of the country and its people. Pure geography is turned, by imaginative symbiosis, into an iconography of heaven and hell. The mountains, the ravines, the specific towns, gardens and features of the land become pregnant with meaning. These overlapping levels of implication yield themselves only to patient re-reading, for their surface is powerfully evocative in its own circumstantial right.

As well as being his only fully fledged tragedy, which embrace the death of the hero, *Under the Volcano* is Lowry's fullest book. I presents at least four characters who are original, individual and sustain an independent existence. Lowry declared all four to b aspects of himself, and his critics have been a little too ready t accept this authorial judgement unchallenged. Nowhere else in hi novels does he give us genuine alternative points of view; in *Unde the Volcano* both Hugh and Geoffrey are well enough developed t fight for their own particular moral and political corners. Thei lifestyles are well differentiated, although tragically interlocked, an their personalities clearly distinct and psychologically validated. I any one of his heroines is to free him from the accusation that h could not create female characters it must be Yvonne. She may b the most under-estimated of all his character creations. And th middle-ground figures – particularly Laruelle and Vigil – fulfil a enriching function significantly absent in every other one of hi novels. This variety of character interest in *Under the Volcano* make it Lowry's best balanced and most universal book.

It is also his best written work of fiction. The integration o character, style and symbols is brilliantly achieved, allowing ful interplay to the stylistic devices which had been present in embryo i *Ultramarine*. For all the immediacy of passion it evokes there is a sens of controlling discipline about this novel which is lacking elsewher in Lowry; *Under the Volcano* is his least self-indulgent novel.

There are many ways to approach this masterwork. It is eas to get submerged in occult levels of reading where one needs t become a student of the Cabbala, of French symbolism, of Mexica politics, of the German cinema, of supranormal correspondences. T miss any of these completely is to impoverish one's understandin of the novel, but to over-emphasise any single one is to risk bein cut off from its central core of accessible passion, wit and tragi dignity. Essentially an introduction like this can only explore th centre of the novel, in its character interplay, and its relationshi to conventional tragedy, and hope that annotations to other leve of reading can make germane hints and suggestions.

Lowry himself sometimes appeared to deprecate the importanc of 'linear narrative' – of the forward drive of genuinely excitin plot. Several of his longer fictions lack this momentum, but *Und the Volcano* conveys a sense of driving urgency across the time span of the Consul's last tragic day alive. It is a novel in which character, plot, setting, and style all contribute to a passionately felt artistic integrity.

The book is also far more politically aware, critical and balanced than anything else Lowry achieved. He evinced few signs, among his predominantly left-wing contemporaries at Cambridge, of being committed to any specific cause or party, but *Under the Volcano* makes a trenchant and valid comment upon several of the root problems of the late 1930s. Though the setting is the apparently remote Mexico, the presence of fascist vigilante groups, of Weber the gun-running right-wing agitator, of the infiltration of German interests both physical and cultural, and of an anti-British government and police, reminds us how all-embracing is the threat to established values. The approach is singularly unpartisan. Though it is the rightists who destroy Geoffrey, Lowry is balanced in his commentary. Hugh, the 'indoor Marxman', represents the euphoric side of communism, which no more has the author's approval than the other extreme. More than any other British writer in Mexico in the 1930s, Lowry seemed sympathetic to many of the aspirations and policies of the Cardenas government; but his discussion has both reticence and lack of partiality.[15] Though Geoff and Hugh argue politics vehemently, the reader is left to see the schisms between them are expressions of a larger cosmic schism which is rending the fabric of society. The ability to place the personal tragedy of Geoffrey Firmin within the context of the breakdown of order and peace world-wide lends gravity and balance to the book.

Such a concept of the relationship between the personal and the general in *Under the Volcano* sanctions discussion of the book as tragedy. On a personal level we watch the last inevitable stages in the destruction of a charismatic individual. The complex admixture of the admirable, the perverse and the inevitably damned in Geoffrey Firmin makes him very like Marlowe's Dr Faustus – with whom the novel seeks to align him. Like Marlowe's hero the Consul is 'a branch that might have grown full straight', he is a 'learned man', and he is damned to a 'hellish fall' – both literally and metaphorically. He may also remind us of the self-destructive side of King Lear – 'to wilful men, The injuries that they themselves procure, Must be their schoolmasters' – for along with his learning, charm and wit goes a streak of savage self-debasement. Yet equally a core of perverse self-defensive *pride* is at work, which manifests itself principally through sexual jealousy. It is this which comes between Geoff and the healing of all the breaches opened up in his life. He rends and flays the things and the people he loves. Conversely, there are moments when he also manifests a wonderful tenderness, which is among his principal redeeming features.

This personal tragedy is enacted on a stage where a more general collapse is implicit. The world of *Under the Volcano* is on the verge of plunging into global war; even Mexico, so far from the European centre of tension, is permeated and corrupted. The tragedy of this is deepened by the use of the theme of Maximilian and Carlotta who, among other things, demonstrate the inability of the Old World to provide solutions for the New World. Their haunting presence in the background of the book not only enhances the sense of doom surrounding Geoff and Yvonne, but also universalises the tragic sense of humanity being foredoomed, whatever its personal volitions.

Tragedy always implies a sense of choice wrongly directed. Geoffrey is apparently offered a second chance, through the unexpected return of his wife, who has left him after a period in which his compulsive drinking contributed to her infidelity.

For over a year he has longed and prayed for exactly this, but when it happens it is too late. Geoffrey's psyche can no longer cope with redemption. That last day finds him helpless to turn back from a final journey into the jaws of hell. His wit and his charisma retain our affection, but he is a burnt-out case. Alcohol is the outward cause and manifestation of his failure of will. But through the universalising agency of the political substratum of the novel, we are made aware that his spiritual malaise is radical and incurable. Here the novel's many kinds of occult suggestiveness play their part. It is full of strange coincidence, of dimly perceived correspondences, and of supernatural linkages of the personal and the cosmic. Geoff himself has studied cabbalistic magic – another of his Faustian characteristics – and the novel convinces us that there *is* a world outside the merely rational present, and which is bringing pressure to bear upon events in that last day.

Firmin, then, is at the centre of a world totally at odds with itself and now unable to draw back from the brink. As with all tragedy a sense of desolating waste is evoked. But this coexists with admiration for the superior, if arbitrary, spiritual anarchy of the hero. He is a bigger man than those left behind, and for the reader this sense of being cut off from a passing giant is exemplary. We shall not look upon his like again. The eldest hath borne most. In telling his story Lowry certainly extenuates nothing – nor sets down aught in malice, for none of his four central characters is a villain. It requires very discreet handling to make us place this value upon the story of the last day in the life of a masochistic drunk. The saving features of Geoffrey Firmin are his wit, his charm, his learning and his ruined nobility. The 1984 film of *Under the Volcano* directed by John Huston fails noticeably to evoke any of these feelings. The book frightens, but it does not depress. In it we are shown a man ridden by a daemon which impels him towards his downfall. But always there are countervailing qualities which redeem him. Under John Huston's utterly misguided direction Albert Finney was never able to make the Consul seem more than a boorish and self-indulgent swine. There was no deep and mysterious sickness of soul at the basis of Finney's catastrophe as the Consul.

Under the Volcano was nearly ten years in the making. Its genesis is typical of Lowry's creative method. Starting as a short story based upon an incident he had experienced in person, it grew through at least four major redraftings to become an elaborate and intricate structure onto which fresh ideas and themes were constantly being superimposed. Even at the time of publication Lowry was unsatisfied with its state of completeness. Margerie had to force the page proofs from him to prevent further additions being made.

The original short story was eventually published (*Prairie Schooner*, vol.37, no 4, 1963–64, pp.284–300), so the book's process of growth can be traced from its inception. The germ of the novel is the bus ride which now occupies Chapter 8, though neither characterisation nor motivation in this first version bear much consistent relationship to the finished novel. The short story dates from very early 1937, and must have been subjected to immediate augmentation, for both Aiken and Calder-Marshall visiting Lowry later that year claim to have seen a draft of something like 40 000 words. This stage of the work was overtaken by the breakup of Lowry's first marriage, which provided important material for the finished version of the book, both through the character of Yvonne, and the anguish experienced by the husband abandoned in Mexico.

The first full draft seems to have disappeared; a second, completed in Canada by 1940 is still extant, however. By March 1941 a third

version had grown out of this, had been submitted to Harold
Matson, Lowry's literary agent, and had been rejected, on the
grounds that it was too much preoccupied with time, and that
the governing pattern did not emerge with sufficient clarity (*SL*
pp.39–40). Since the handling of time in the finished version is
one of its strongest features, and a principal contributor to the
clarity of the overall pattern, it is clear that major revision
now supervened. This restructuring seems to have occupied Lowry
immediately and extensively, for by September 1941 the manuscript
had been submitted and rejected yet again. Still undaunted, though
obviously tortured by frustration and disappointment, Lowry set
about yet another major reworking, which occupied him through
to Christmas 1944.

Another way of exploring the tortuous gestation of the book
is through the monumental letter to Jonathan Cape which Lowry
wrote in the days following 2 January 1946, after receiving from
Cape an intimation that the book was possibly going to be rejected
yet again. This letter constitutes a critique of supreme importance
to understanding *Under the Volcano*. Chapter by chapter, image by
image, hour by hour, Lowry justifies what he has written against the
threat of having it cut. Everyone who writes on the novel essentially
weaves new patterns around the exegesis Lowry himself presents. He
superannuated his critics even before they existed. It is one of the
most remarkable critical documents of this century, emanating an
assured sense of authority, responsibility, and patience in mediating
between the text and a sceptical reader.

Among other things this letter describes when and how the work
was revised. For instance, of Chapter 3 Lowry says 'This was first
written in 1940, and completed in 1942'. Presumably this means that,
apart from adding in motifs which had developed in other chapters,
he was satisfied with the overall design and contents of this chapter
well before the date of final completion for the book in 1944.

Chapter 5 goes all the way back to 1937, and its final revisions
were made in March 1943. Chapter 6 had an even more complex
evolution:

The middle part of the shaving scene was written in 1937,
as was the very end, that much comprising the whole chapter
then. The new version was done in 1943 but I had not quite
finally revised it in 1944 when my house burned down. The

final revisions I made later in 1944 comprised the first work I had been able to do since the fire, in which several pages of this chapter and notes for cuts were lost . . . (*SL*, pp.76–7)

Chapter 7 was first written in 1936, and underwent numerous rewritings in 1937, 1940, 1941, 1943, and finally 1944: Chapter 8 comprised the 'original germ' but it was not until a 1941 revision that the fascist deputies first appeared. Given their importance in the final plot, this seems extraordinary, if characteristic. Chapter 9 underwent three major revisions, which altered the narratorial stance. In 1937 it was told through Hugh's eyes; it was then redrafted as though told by Geoffrey, and finally took shape as Yvonne's chapter. Complete in 1944, its period of gestation was thus the longest for any chapter in the book. Chapter 10 also had a lengthy history, and must have been among the last parts of the book revised late in 1944. Chapter 11 emerged as the very last one written, though it has been averred that Yvonne's dying vision of being drawn upwards to the stars is actually a fossil remnant of a very early version where the same description depicts her adulterous passion with Hugh!

The last chapter dates back originally to 1937, and, says the author, has been scarcely changed since 1940, save for minor alterations in 1942, and one piece of tinkering in 1944.

This fragmentary and non-consecutive process of composing, reworking and joining up the story is typical. The inexorable coherence of the finished book is the more remarkable, given its vexed history of composition. The process implies an author for whom surface story-line is not the most important thing. This is still the Lowry of *Ultramarine*, albeit now infinitely more skilful, complex and passionate. For Lowry story-line is the point of impact at which the stone hits the surface of the water. What really fascinates him is watching the complex pattern of related ripples which move outward from that point. To any novelist with this method of story-telling the long period of revising, redrafting and reconsidering may well be advantageous, however much hardship is involved. Of course there comes a point where this constant thickening of texture will overload the fabric. The density of *Under the Volcano* is enormously exciting; it is fascinating to discover that the sign in the public garden, of which so much pregnant use is made in the novel, was added in at the very last moment. How

could anything so seminal to the entire fabric have appeared so lat
in the day?

The coincidences and traumas which beset Lowry at the tim
of the final acceptance of *Under the Volcano* belong to the chapte
on *Dark as the Grave*, a novel about a writer revisiting Mexico wher
he had earlier written a long-rejected novel, which is now finall
accepted. This reflects what happened in reality, when in Apri
1946, during a much troubled holiday showing Margerie the sight
of Cuernavaca and Oaxaca, Lowry finally heard that the book wa
accepted, without further revision, both in England and America
Typically the news broke in the midst of such appalling hassle witl
the Mexican immigration authorities that the joy of publication afte
ten whole years of rejection was scarcely felt at all. A poem 'Afte
Publication of *Under the Volcano*' affirms feelings quite the reverse o
triumphant:

> Success is like some horrible disaster
> Worse than your house burning, the sounds of ruination
> As the rooftree falls following each other faster
> While you stand, the helpless witness of your damnation.
> Fame, like a drunkard consumes the house of the soul
> Exposing that you have worked for only this –
> Ah, that I had never suffered this treacherous kiss
> And had been left in darkness for ever to founder and fall.[16]

This is tragically prophetic. The richly deserved success of *Unde
the Volcano* became a burden Lowry found hard to live with. He wa
so shy, or at least so bad in crowds, that he could not cope with th
fêteing and junketing which engulfed him as a newly famous author
More horribly, he became haunted by the plight of a man who i
unable to repeat or build upon his success – the fear of being a
one-book author who can do nothing but go on writing; writing
about an author who fears he is a one-book author. This is th
very special kind of hell he hints at in *Dark as the Grave* certainly
though *October Ferry* has, for all its other faults, apparently purge
itself of this fear at least. But the self-consciousness of Lowry'
creative stance in the early 1950s genuinely seems to spring from
a fear that he has written the one great book he had in him. I
fact the triumph of *Under the Volcano* is partly the distance from
himself that Lowry manages to create. The more introspectively

autobiographical he subsequently became, the more incestuous did his fiction appear.

Composed by a method which creates layers or strata of meaning, *Under the Volcano* requires explanation by a process which recognises these levels. The symbols and icons such as the garden, the barranca, the mountains, the fiesta, permeate through these strata and bind them into a unity which accretes around the story-line itself. Stripped of its intensifying detail the plot sounds melodramatic. Both the conviction and the poetry of the book stem from its accretions.

The plot of *Under the Volcano* is infinitely more rich and exciting than that of *Ultramarine*. The persons involved are experienced adults whose destinies are capable of evoking genuine pity and commitment. The settings are brilliantly evoked and varied, and the interplay of politics and private passion well managed. The accretions of symbolic detail are fully integrated into the plot; they always augment and explain, but seldom obtrude. All these are manifest signs of progress from Lowry's first novel.

The greatest advance is the intellectual capacity and the worldly experience of its central figure. This transcends development in Lowry himself such as we might expect between the late 1920s and the mid 1940s. Geoffrey Firmin represents an imaginative achievement of real substance; all the other Lowry protagonists are little men by contrast with him.

It is a truism of Lowry criticism, emanating from the author himself, that he had no gift for characterisation – that all his heroes are versions of himself. He certainly did not often invent rounded and individuated figures who differ radically from what he himself was like. But in *Under the Volcano* he transcended his limitation. The Consul is a wonderfully complex, dynamic and consistent creation. He has tragic dignity, even when he is at his most perverse. He can be weak, irresponsible, often downright cruel, sometimes dishonest. Yet he remains truly the centre of sympathy in the book whose tendency is to make us feel awe and pity for him.

If all four main characters are aspects of Lowry, he has contrived the debate and the tensions between them with extraordinary discretion and no little skill. What one feels about them is a sense of distinctness. Laruelle is fussy, precise, creative in a slightly effete way. Hugh is superdynamic, brash, a quixotic doer of flamboyant deeds. Geoffrey is a mixture of diffidence and superiority; clearly the most intellectual of the characters, there are hints that in his

past he may also have been the most genuinely active. His point
of view transcend and make look callow those of all the other
and his compulsion for self-destruction adds a sense of tragi
mystery to him. Thus to whatever extent all these may represen
'the abominable author' he has here created and sustained vali
dramatic distinctions. The sense of his menfolk having a degree o
autonomous life contributes largely to the success of the book.

The distinctions are carried right back into the documente
childhoods of each. It is Laruelle, in Chapter 1, who recalls th
boyhood of both Geoffrey and himself, two lonely and out-of-plac
lads in the heavy-drinking and hearty Taskerson household. The
early brushes with both sex and drink are germane to the characte
they develop as adults. In retrospect a poignancy is added to th
novel when we appreciate that Laruelle, in Chapter 1, is reflectin
back upon a dead man whom he has wronged, and who had n
cause to have loved him. Yet Laruelle regrets Geoff's passing wit
real vehemence. He leads what is virtually a chorus of regret i
that opening movement of the tragedy, supported by Sr Bustament
and Dr Vigil. It is cardinally important that this elegaic mood i
established before we meet Geoff himself. In excising Laruell
altogether the film of *Under the Volcano* committed a cardinal error.

The character interrelationships continue to throw up intriguin
points of overlap and divergence between the principal male
Geoff and Jacques share certain adolescent experiences. Both ar
interested in the history and ethnography of Mexico. Both are o
have been passionately committed to Yvonne. Both are about to tur
their backs on Mexico in varieties of abdication. Yet the difference
are substantial. Jacques is a hoarder of artifacts, Geoff a kind o
collector of people; he relates to the ordinary folk of Mexico fa
more deeply than any of the other characters, and is the only on
who can elicit a response from them. Despite Laruelle's creativit
as a film-maker, one feels he is less deeply committed to humanit
than Geoff. He is strongly marked by a rather prissy liking fo
routine and order. Nothing could contrast more strongly with th
heroic shambles that Geoff leaves in his wake.

Hugh is all assertiveness. His manner of arriving in Mexico -
stowed away in the back of a cattle-truck – his breezy confidenc
which covers boyish insecurity, the uncertainty of his basic attitudes
all these make him utterly different from his elder half-brother
Again they share the common background of deprived childhood

indeed, Geoff virtually acted as father-substitute to Hugh. They are bound to the same woman. Geoff's reaction to Hugh is a beautiful mixture of paternal tenderness, vehement bitterness to a betrayer, and warm consanguinity. Some of the novel's most sharply observed moments are those where Geoff and Hugh are together. To argue that they are joint parts of a single character – the author – may be true and valuably true up to a point. But it is likely to blind us to some of Lowry's strongest writing as he shapes the *distinctions* between these two who are so naturally close. The bitterness of their political divisions seems to stem as much from temperamental affinities as from ideological divisions. Yet it is Hugh's offhandedness and carelessness that finally destroys Geoff. He leaves his contentious telegram in the pocket of the jacket he had borrowed from Geoff, and when the vigilantes search Geoff at the Farolito he is too drunk to convince them that he is not the pro-communist author of this document.

We learn a good deal about Hugh's background. Some of it is based upon the early Lowry – the song writing, the sea voyage. But the *treatment* of these flakes of biography is highly imaginative, and totally integrated into the fabric of the novel. The fact that so much of Hugh's adolescent posturing makes Geoffrey (and himself) wince adds a savour to these episodes. It also strongly suggests that Lowry is able to transcend the image of himself in immaturity, and to hold a critical balance which strengthens his characters, however close to himself they may be in their inception. The tensions between the males in the book are dynamic, meaningful and subtly recorded.

Lowry's declared weakness with female characters is surely less evident in *Under the Volcano* than in any of his other writing. Yvonne is said to be a composite study of both the real Lowry wives. Margerie always spoke deprecatingly of Yvonne as inconsistent – starting out horrid (that is, as Jan, the first wife), and becoming more sympathetic (as herself?). Until Gordon Bowker's compilation did any justice to Jan she remained a slightly shadowy figure placed only by Margerie's remarks. She can now be seen in much more sharp-edged clarity. The real gain has surely been, not in the points battle between the two real wives, but in our ability to see Yvonne as a character of some originality and distinction.

As with the other principal characters her childhood is carefully sketched in. She has been involved in the Hollywood film industry since childhood, and had to support a feckless tragi-comic father. She

shares things in common with Geoff and Hugh here, for their father
simply walked off one morning to find Shangri-La the in high
Himalayas. Mr Constable has made a mess of everything from wire-
fence manufacture to pineapple cultivation, and Yvonne is scarred
by her early experiences. A good deal of the blame is taken off her
subsequent actions. She has certainly betrayed and failed Geoff,
but her own psychic mutilation calls for pity and understanding.
Although she has committed adultery twice between her marriage
to Geoff in 1936 and his death in November 1938 it is hard to blame
her completely. Geoff's drink fixation, his volatile moods and his
inability to sustain the responsibility of a full relationship make her
a poignant figure. We are given further exoneration of Yvonne; she
is wounded by a previous farcical Hollywood marriage to a playboy
millionaire and by the loss of her only child. She probably now
requires exactly the kind of care and tenderness which Geoff is
incapable of providing. Again, this degree of creative sympathy with
one of his female characters is quite untypical of Lowry's writing.

Yvonne's courage and persistence on that last day are admirable.
Having bravely decided to return, despite Geoff ignoring her letters,
she is determined that this last chance shall not fail for lack of her
effort. The situation is made much worse for her by the accidental
presence of Hugh, but she copes with this unwanted embarrassment
with grace and tact. She is true to her purpose despite Geoff's
repertoire of unwarranted and sometimes downright vicious attacks.
She manifestly stands, as a character, head and shoulders above
Janet in *Ultramarine* and equally above the fussy mother-hen figures
of *Dark as the Grave* and *October Ferry*. The assumption that there is
no depth of individuality to the characters other than the Consul
in *Under the Volcano* is a critical error of some magnitude.

When all has been said about the other characters, however, the
essence of the tragedy inheres in the character of Geoffrey Firmin.
He does not appear in Chapter 1, but is always at its centre as other
people recall him and build an atmosphere. Each of the 'minor'
characters bears testimony to the charm, the charisma and the
misfortune of the Consul. This is supported by the narrative evidence
of Geoff's childhood and upbringing. Disparate and varied factors
are produced which elicit pity for him. His childhood was broken by
parental irresponsibility, yet something of his father's individualistic
irresponsibility may be present in Geoff too. Responsibility is cruelly
thrust on him at too early an age; he has to act as father-substitute

for Hugh. His sojourn with the colourful Taskersons does nothing
to alleviate his loneliness and inability to come to terms with the
world around him. The Taskersons episode also fills in detail on
Geoff's adult attitude to sexuality. It is, ironically, Laruelle, who
stumbles on Geoff with a girl in the 'Hell Bunker' on the Leasowe
golf course, at a highly compromised but unfulfilled stage of physical
involvement. From this time it seems Geoff is unable to make normal
sexual adjustments. This will haunt the relationship he has with
Yvonne. Failed friendship and stultified sexuality are closely aligned.
Jacques had been brought from France in the hope of providing companionship more to Geoff's taste than that of the muscular Taskerson
boys. But 'the holiday fizzled out in desolation and equinoctial gales.
It had been a melancholy dreary parting . . .' (p.27). This is the only
schoolboy friendship the Consul can remember. It is not surprising
that adult relationships do not come easily to him; nor that in later
life he should be distrustful of Jacques when they meet again in
Mexico, and Yvonne stands between them.

Much is done to exonerate or at least to explain his alcoholic
compulsion – vital if we are to retain sympathy with the anti-social
and indulgent conduct this produces in the main part of the story.
Chapter 1 makes it quite clear that his drinking is an illness, not
merely an indulgence.

It is worth noting that Geoff comes from India along with
Hugh; this sense of the tragedy spreading world-wide is underlined
by the backgrounds of Jacques and Yvonne too. This expansiveness
or inclusiveness is unlike the atmosphere in most of Lowry's novels.
The opening paragraphs of the book, which read almost like a
guidebook, are intentional. This is not just the tragedy of an obscure
ex-consul in central America. He genuinely comes to represent a
global malaise.

It is the charming Mexican, Dr Vigil, who speaks the simple
but moving epitaph which, summing up his feelings for Geoff, also
introduces the terminology of tragedy into the book:

> Sickness is not only in body, but in that part used to be
> call: soul. Poor your friend he spend his money on earth in
> such continuous tragedies. (p.11)

Like so much in Chapter 1 this establishes an ambience essential
if we are to see the main story as tragedy rather than melodrama.

Lowry then ties his own tragic tale to a cognate one from the actua
history of Mexico: the utterly sad story of Maximilian and Carlotta
Scarcely perceptible dislocations of time associate the words and th
identities of Geoff and Yvonne with those of the Emperor and hi
wife who were betrayed by the European establishment, and the
misjudged and murdered by Mexicans with whom, but for politica
ironies and exigencies, they might have had a natural affinity.

Chapter 1 also sketches in Geoff's failure as a professiona
man. He seems to have been a pretty lamentable Consul, partl
because he has a wry humour which transcends national identit
and makes it difficult for him to take the job seriously. Britai
and Mexico were practically at war in the late 1930s, and bot
Lowry and his character seem to have had an unfashionable, bu
justifiable, sympathy with the Mexican side of the argument. (Th
interested reader will find a startlingly partial account of the othe
side in Evelyn Waugh's *Robbery Under Law*, published in 1939.) Th
ordinary Mexicans with whom Geoff has been in contact all hav
a singular affection for him, epitomised by Bustamente and Vigi
but extending to many of the beggars and lay figures who inhab
the novel's periphery. This feeling, never over-stated, but alway
present, is of the greatest importance in guiding and directing th
reader's response to Geoffrey Firmin as tragic hero. Whatever othe
advantages accrue from setting the opening chapter a year on in tim
from the main story, one of the most important and least emphasise
is this atmosphere of sympathy.

Unlike most of the foreigners who come and go through th
book – Jacques, Hugh, Yvonne, Weber – Geoff has surrogat
roots in Mexico. The real contrast comes from a comic episode i
Chapter 3 where a passing Englishman, claiming to be from Caiu
but wearing a Trinity tie, patronises and is utterly bewildered b
Geoff, who is lying drunk in the street in front of his car. Geoff a
the Englishman 'gone native' and letting the side down, comicall
invites us to see things from a non-establishment view point.

There is another side to Geoff, however. Lowry finds time i
this extraordinarily dense opening chapter to sketch in his wa
experiences. He may now be a superannuated consul in a backwate
but he has been something of a war hero. Whether or not his crew di
burn their German captives in the submarine-hunter's furnaces w
can never quite work out. The point seems to be that Geoff himse

may now have doubts about it. He seems prepared to think the worst of himself all the time and thus carries a burden of guilt about the war. Not surprising that 'His life had become a quixotic oral fiction . . . he had become rather careless of his honour . . .' (p.39). Thus is introduced the major running motif of Geoffrey's identification with Faustus, carried forward by much of the later icon-making. Faustus, after all, is the most wilful of tragic heroes, and thus the most appropriate to be identified with Lowry's protagonist.

Faustus was a 'learned man'; this becomes a keynote of Geoffrey's character as the book unfolds and we witness the marvellous if muddled complexity of his frame of reference. No other character in the book approaches Geoffrey's ability to cross the boundaries of ideas.

Chapter 1 also introduces us to the sensitive, lyrical side of his nature – something which his last day alive in Chapters 2 to 12 will have little scope to do. The letter found by Laruelle in the book of plays (which significantly includes *Faustus*) is that of an alienated and haunted poet. Geoffrey writes of '. . . the howling pariah dogs, the cocks that herald dawn all night . . . the eternal sorrow that never sleeps of great Mexico!' (p.41). This lyrical element supports the feeling of tragedy as does the portentous imminence of 'horrors portioned to a giant nerve', and the Consul's sadly unavailing self-knowledge.

> I sometimes thinks of myself, as a great explorer who has discovered some extraordinary land from which he can never return to give his knowledge to the world: but the name of this land is hell. (pp.41–2)

The Consul's letter superficially holds up any narrative development, but tonally is of great importance. It is the letter of a man already dead; all its aspirations and passion come to us from beyond the grave. Geoff writes of needing help 'across this abyss of my life', but anyone beyond their first reading knows that he has already foundered in the abyss. He pleads that without Yvonne's help he will fall. The terminology is again redolent with irony.

We also learn that his malady is in part the medieval sin of acedia: utterly enervating moral torpor. His confession of inability to contact Yvonne (p.44) underlines the hideous nature of the cause and effect of

self-destruction within him. No careful reader of Chapter 1 probabl
expects things to work out even when Yvonne does return. Whil
most critics recognise the importance of this chapter in establishin
Time in the novel, fewer have been prepared to acknowledge it as th
cornerstone of character.

From the framework here provided, the living portrait of th
Consul is built up in later chapters. The case against him is strongl
stated during that last day. He can be selfish, indulgent, wilful, cruel
jealous, masochistic. Only through Chapter 1 are we able to redres
this balance and see him as a man worth redeeming but now beyon
redemption.

No other figure in the book matches him for grace, natura
authority and outgoing human sympathy. He can manifest a touch
ing tenderness, and assume a quixotic concern for the cosmi
problems of mankind. We learn, for instance, how a derange
beggar took him for Christ himself. Grimly ironic as this ma
be it moves our sympathy and respect. Geoff is followed aroun
by a series of cringing pariah dogs during that last day. Whil
these echo his own forlorn and abandoned state, his care toward
them is moving. 'Yet this day, *pichicho*, shalt thou be with me i
– ' he begins to address one such beast, following Christ's word
to the felon alongside him on Calvary (p.232). Motifs of this kin
control and direct our overall impression of the Consul. He is a
extraordinarily un-class-conscious man; this is rare among Lowry'
protagonists, most of whom are obtrusively middle class. It i
a manifestation of his largeness of spirit that Geoffrey Firmi
transcends this limitation.

Lowry hated people to underrate the quality and extent of th
comedy in *Under the Volcano*. The final tragic grandeur of the novel i
depreciated if its moments of farce, of wit, and of intellectual bravur
are undervalued. High farce is present in the fairground episode a
Geoff is whirled round and inverted on the Cocteau-esque inferna
machine. There are ferocious undertones both in the symbolism an
within the surface plot, but the *absurdity* of the moment is excellentl
realised. Equally, the marvellous innocence with which Geoffre
stands open-flyed before his prissy next-door neighbour, attemptin
Consular gravity, is beautifully achieved. His ability with words i
equally striking and often embraces outrageous shades of humour.

Whatever is said about his culpability in creating the state he ha
reached, it is impossible to avoid pity for the ruin of a noble min

which has been reduced to helplessness. His moral responsibility is lessened by the phantasmagoric and fleeting attention he is able to pay to the simple stream of reality which passes him by on that last day. Critics argue about the extent to which he is being spied upon and manipulated. The suggestions seem very strong. The novel is full of dark corners, just out of focus where men in dark glasses are peering out at Geoff, where the fascist auxiliaries are permanently suspicious, but perhaps ill-informed enough to get the wrong Firmin at the end. The possibility of this malign world being always present just out of frame adds substantially to the terror. Nobody else seems aware of the danger; Geoff is beyond caring. His desire for damnation takes on an air of inevitability. And while Time, as Lowry's structure insists, is keeping one inexorable rhythm, hour by hour, chapter by chapter, through that last day, Geoffrey refuses to be constrained by it. Equally he is the only person in the book whose mind reaches out to the metaphysical.

Geoffrey doing nothing is far more interesting that Hugh in all his ebullient antics – swimming, planning to climb the volcano, riding through the gardens. These physical activities are reduced to triviality by the quality of Geoff's intellectual activity.

It is difficult to say how seriously we are to take Geoff's role as a failed magician. Assuredly he is the only man in the book of whom we could remotely believe it. The motif is powerful but patchily sustained alongside the Faustus theme. It helps us to see him as a fine but wayward intellect; his library is stuffed full of esoterica, and he dabbles in the Cabbala. Since the entire universe is filled that last day with weird correspondences and coincidences, perhaps we are meant to see Geoff, like Faustus, as a man living in a haunted universe whose own magical powers have deserted him. It is part of cabbalistic lore that alcohol abuse takes power from the adept.

In his ending pity and fear once more cohere. Why will he not stop drinking? Why will he not save himself? Why do Hugh and Yvonne fail to arrive in time to intervene? The last chapter of the novel was Lowry's favourite; it is easy to see why. It has authority in shape, texture and movement. It is highly charged, yet there is space for a last wilful arabesque of self-destruction through Geoff's coupling with the prostitute, Maria. There is no sentimentalising of the self-creating victim here. And how well Lowry manages the quality of the dialogue which washes around Geoffrey's fitful

attention as he stands at the bar in the Farolito. This intermitten
fleeting drunkard's concentration is superbly recorded, and the cross
fading and the cutting of visual and aural effects is of the highes
order. Running alongside the urgent tragedy there is evoked an awfu
comic version of the Tower of Babel, through the frantic stool-pigeo
and the mysterious old woman. Truly the world seems to be goin
mad here. Lay figures from the corners of the canvas jerk into life

Finally, the brutality, the cold collected horror of the force
which oppose him are underlined. The mad titles of Authority
chief of Rostrums, Chief of Gardens – are surrealistic but poten
It is difficult to read the novel's last few pages without a sens
of disbelief that these comic opera banditti are really capable c
destroying Geoffrey. Perhaps the novel's most fearful use of dramati
irony suddenly rushes out to assail one. The two chief policemen ar
called Sanabria and Zuzugoita – the very names which had leaped a
random off the page of the telephone directory at Geoff in Laruelle'
apartment earlier (p.212). If awful coincidence has reached this stag
then the world truly is the haunt of malevolent spirits. This i
closely coupled with the irony whereby we realise that in his las
moments Geoffrey has released the horse which has caused th
death of Yvonne.

There remains to discuss the problem of *time* in *Under the Volcan*
Jonathan Cape's reader objected to the time structure whereb
Chapter 1 occurs a year later than the principal events of the mai
plot. Much of the above discussion on character has intentionall
also been a defence of this chapter. Beyond the boundaries alread
proposed Lowry himself recognised the objections which might wel
be raised to a method which inevitably discusses a character befor
he appears and expects us to have knowledge of events we hav
not yet witnessed. The 'flashback' is a cinematographic stereotype
Lowry foresaw the objections to it in his novel. He countered thes
objections in his famous letter to Cape:

> . . . I suggest that whether or not the *Volcano* as it is seem
> tedious at the beginning depends somewhat upon . . . (the) . .
> reader's state of mind, and how prepared he is to grapple wit
> the form of the book and the author's true intention. (*SL*, p.58)

His hope is that, rhythmically, Chapter 1 establishes the slov
sadness of Mexico itself, and places this in dynamic context. Thu

also he establishes the global points of reference already discussed as germane to the central characters; he creates an ambience stretching from India to Hawaii and the Far East. He is trying to lay down themes and tone which can be taken up later. He is *consciously* thwarting the reader's natural desire to indulge a linear approach to the story. Chapter 1 helps to emphasise that *Under the Volcano* is not simply or primarily the factitious and historical narrative of Geoffrey Firmin's last day alive. Indeed, Lowry suggests that the novel should be read 'vertically' rather than 'horizontally'. The analogy is familiar enough in music; it challenges us to accept a radical concept of form and material in the novel.

He is out to create resonant themes, not principally to elucidate plot. Indeed the first-time reader probably has no more idea about what is really happening on the surface at the end of Chapter 1 than he had at the beginning. The final authorial defence of this is that 'new meanings will certainly reveal themselves . . . (to the reader) . . . if he reads this book again'. Many people find this is true. The book continues to yield new insights after the twentieth let alone after the second reading and Chapter 1, for all its obliquity of approach, falls into place.

The novel's time scheme is observed with punctilious care. The problem is that several senses of time coexist and overlap. Because of the flashback technique the whole thing is set in a cocoon of time past. For Geoff the clock has been running since the night before (he has been up all night at the Red Cross Ball); for Yvonne the clock is turned back as she returns, and her sense of time is dislocated by her long journey. Geoff is given a chance to resume a life-rhythm he has abjured since Yvonne's departure, but he is incapable of doing so. His last day proceeds in jerks and rushes as he alternates between hyperactivity and blackout. For Hugh and Yvonne time passes at a much smoother and apparently quieter logical pace.

Other wheels and circles of time are implied. The novel opens on 2 November 1939. This is the Day of the Dead in Mexico; the ironic significance soon emerges. It is precisely twelve months since the day of the death of the Consul. Even the unseasonable weather repeats itself, and the actions of Vigil and Laruelle echo what happened twelve months previously. In Chapter 1 Laruelle is looking back not only across that crucial twelve months, but across longer vistas of Geoffrey's past, to the time when coincidence brought them together as children, as it has done again now they are adults.

His own timescale will limp forward into the future – he is about to leave Quauhnahuac. What his future holds for him is obscure. He is going back to France, where war is about to engulf the country. As in most Lowry novels the future is cut off completely.

At the end of the chapter the symbolic ferris wheel is deployed to sweep time one full circle backwards to 7 a.m. on 2 November 1938. Throughout that day Lowry keeps surface time with the peremptory authority of a French classical tragedian. But alternative time scales and values constantly cross-cut the linear strand which moves the plot forward. Chapter 4, for instance, is a pastoral idyll. Hugh and Yvonne ride out into the countryside. This is the novel's most peaceful and calm-spirited chapter. There appears to be no pressure of time upon the characters at all. Geoff is asleep – time is passing him by. Hugh and Yvonne pick their lazy way through the remnants of Maximilian's hunting park, deliberately stave off talking about their mutual past, and plan a hypothetical future for the absent Geoff. In the background we are dimly aware of the time past of Maximilian, the apparently timeless world of the brewery episode, and the curiously exploited time implicit in the deliberately winding railroad built by the British. Such alternative times complicate the narrative thread at many points in the story.

In Chapters 11 and 12, time, like the forest paths the characters are treading, bifurcates. Lowry's problem is that Geoff and Yvonne die within minutes of each other, but are physically separated. His solution is to overlap time. Geoff's situation is held in abeyance while we follow Yvonne and Hugh in their vain pursuit of him. In fact, the matter of Chapter 12 is occurring at precisely the same time. This is what Lowry meant by 'vertical' reading of the novel. They miss rescuing Geoff by exactly the time it takes them to have one last drink at the 'El Popo'.

Chapter 11 is the other strand of this bifurcation of time. The poignancy is only manifest to a reader who knows the plot already.

Keeping strict time is one thing, but as Lowry elaborates his linear plot so he creates other alternative times in each chapter. He explores the past of each character at some length; Hugh's adolescence, Geoff's war years, Yvonne's precocious childhood all weave across simple time present. Time future is much less certain. Occasionally the 'northern paradise' is evoked – an alternative world where Geoff and Yvonne can escape from Mexico and into the future. But from reading Chapter 1 we know that time future is irrevocably sealed off from Geoff. These alternative scales of time are part of Lowry's technique for creating density and vertical depth to the experience described in the novel.

A survey of this kind inevitably undervalues or misses out aspects of so complex a novel. Hopefully, clear perspectives emerge from an approach which tries to go no further than discussing salient features of character, structure and plot shape. The following notes are intended as further guides to the novel. The structure of sustained symbols which underpins the plot may require exegesis, and the minor icons require pointing up. The fullest account of the novel's machinery is the admirable *Companion to 'Under the Volcano'* by C. Ackerley and J. Clipper (Vancouver, UBC Press, 1984). This is not always readily accessible to British readers, however, and it is hoped that the following material will clarify some of the dense texture of *Under the Volcano*.

NOTES ON THE MAIN RECURRING SYMBOLS AND THE PRINCIPAL ICONS IN *Under the Volcano*

The main symbols are those which recur consistently throughout the novel. The casual icons are those poetically enhancing details which create specific parallelisms, but which are static and do not recur. Conjointly they are vital parts of Lowry's plan for the novel – his 'chirrugueresque cathedral', as he called it. They are listed consecutively as they occur; page references are to the Penguin text (1963).

p.9 – *cantinas*
These have a hierarchy of horror or malevolence, as well as literal differences of function. Thus a pulquería serves mainly *pulque* – one of the less lethal Mexican drinks – and, incidentally, one the Consul (who shares this taste with his author) doesn't like.

The names of these various pubs, bars, taverns, hotels and restaurants are often mordantly significant. 'La Selva' and 'El Bosque' both mean 'the wood' and refer covertly to the Dante-esque level of the novel, underlined by Hugh quoting *The Inferno*, by the concept of the Consul as a wanderer seeking his destiny, and by the tutelary figure of Vigil, who presumably equates tangentially – and ironically – to Dante's Virgil.

The entire day is a progress towards the final bar, the Farolito
at Parián. Lowry himself said Parián equals death. 'Farolito' in
Spanish means, literally, 'the little lighthouse'; thus it beckons
Geoffrey with an insidious and inverted attraction, to death rather
than safety. But the word 'farol' can also mean 'delusion'; thus there
is always a built-in pun/warning as the Consul talks of finding his
way there.

The owners of the various cantinas are key minor characters
in the book. Señora Gregorio, for instance, at times reminds the
Consul, through his drunken apocalyptic vision, of his mother
Diosdado (the God-given) of the Farolito is conversely ominous
and remote, an Authority/father figure. And the malign effect of
cantinas upon Geoffrey is wonderfully contrasted in Chapter 4 with
the Cervecería (brewery) which Yvonne and Hugh discover on their
horse-ride, serving refreshing and innocuous beer rather than the
spirits which destroy Geoffrey.

The theme of drinking places as mileposts on the road to hell had
begun for the Consul in his youth, when, after his sexual humiliation
in being caught *in flagrante delicto* in the 'hell bunker' by Laruelle, he
went off to a nearby pub called 'The Case is Altered'.

gardens
Lowry quickly establishes the outward picturesqueness of Quauhnahuac (Cuernavaca) as a town of gardens. They are a contrast
with the state of nature represented by forest, jungle, desert and
wilderness which occupy those parts of Mexico which have not been
tamed; and (by implication) they sustain the motif of Dante's wood
The Garden of Eden itself is hinted at; on one level the Consul is
Adam – archetypal sinning man, misled by his own will (just as on
other levels he is Faustus and Prometheus.)

We quickly learn that, amidst all the prosperous middle-class
gardens of the attractive town, the Consul's garden has 'run to
seed. Things rank and gross in nature possess it merely' (*Hamlet*). It
symbolises the way Geoffrey himself has gone to seed since Yvonne
left, and the rather sporadic attempts that she and Hugh make to
repair the damage by weeding and rearranging shadow their efforts
to redeem Geoffrey.

The Firmins' garden is surrounded by contrasts. On one side lies
the antiseptic neatness of the garden of Quincey, their neighbour.
The contrast between his manicured patch and the briar-ridden

wilderness on Geoffrey's side of the fence is very potent. On another side of the Consul's garden lies the barranca, the malign symbol of destruction and dark natural anarchy (q.v.). And on the other boundary runs a public garden which is being carefully tended – and in which is the signboard which Geoffrey so potently mistranslated. There is even a snake in Geoffrey's inverted Eden – whether real or dreamed up by his drink-phantasms is of no matter. This in itself is echoed in Chapter 4 by the dead snake Hugh rides over when he and Yvonne are out. And, of course, they ride through the pleasantly reconstructed outworks of Maximilian's pleasure gardens in the book's one therapeutic chapter. Hugh's snake, among other things, represents the suppression of his guilty desire for Yvonne; the whole chapter is an idyll of release – 'a necessary ozone' – as Lowry put it, in the prevailing gloom. The notice in the public garden (*vide* note on p.132) and its mistranslated message are repeated frequently. Lowry (*SL*, p.74) calls it 'the most important theme in the book'.

Beyond this, on the political level, Lowry was very sympathetic to the Cardenas government's attempted land redistribution through credit facilities to peasant farmers, and the idea of the well-tended state unravaged by the internal dissentions of rival ideologies offers further parallels with the personal problems of the ravaged Consul. (cf. also the note, pp.16 and 18, on *the two Palaces*.)

p.9 – *the Day of the Dead*
November 2 is celebrated as a fiesta in Mexico. The Mexican attitude to death may bewilder Europeans: elaborate tombs, lavishly decorated, where families go for a picnic; funerals where – just as described on p.61 – a child's obsequies are accompanied by a band playing *La Cucaracha*; the public sale of chocolate sweetmeats in the form of coffins and skeletons. This background creates local colour for Lowry, and provides a prevailing current of irony to his tragedy. It is a day when one is supposed to obtain plenary indulgence by visiting church and saying prayers for the dead. The Consul's taverna visits are an inversion of this idea. Also, on 2 November the souls of the dead are supposed to return; it is the night that Geoffrey is sent *from* this world. And after precisely one year Laruelle is finally going away because he realises Geoffrey can't be 'brought back'.

The idea of contrasting Geoff's downward path to death against the annually returning festival celebrating a victory over death is arresting. Lowry himself first arrived in Mexico on 2 November!

Popocatapetl and Ixtaccihuatl

These two volcanoes physically dominate Quauhnahuac. On a literal
level life in the town *is* lived 'under the volcano'. The ancients placed
hell beneath a volcano, and Lowry was quick to see the metaphoric
value of geography; wherever his characters move they are followed
by the shapes of the mountain peaks.

The old Mexican Indian folklore about the mountains is also
invoked. Popocatapetl represents the male principle: the story
has it that he was a warrior who fell in love with the female
archetype Ixtaccihuatl. But their love was thwarted at the moment
of consummation and Ixtaccihuatl was lost to him. Now, eternally,
the smoking peak of the male warrior-lover stands guarding the
quiescent breast-shaped mound of his bride. When, on p.97 therefore, the Consul calls Ixtaccihuatl and Popocatapetl 'the image of
the perfect marriage' there is a cataclysmic irony. For Geoffrey has
just failed to make physical love to Yvonne and the transference of
the dormancy of the mounts to his own drink-induced impotence is
most poignant.

As the tragic end of the novel draws near in Chapters 11 and
12 so do the shapes of the two volcanoes come more and more
obtrusively to dominate the texture of the writing.

pp.16 and 18 – the two Palaces

The principal public building in Quauhnahuac is the Cortez Palace
where Diego Rivera's murals are located. Rivera (1886–1957) is probably Mexico's greatest artist. A liberal, he specialised in huge-scale
depictions of the dignity and travail of the ordinary people of
Mexico, and in left-wing accounts of its history. The Cortez Palace
mural depicts the conquest of Mexico. The cover to the Penguin
edition (1963) of *Under the Volcano* is a fair representation of his
chunky and loaded style, with which Lowry's vision has a kinship.

The fresco is invoked several times. But it is the other Palace in
Quauhnahuac which interested Lowry most – the ruined hunting-
lodge of the tragic and ill-fated Maximilian (q.v.). The remnants of
the estate he laid out in the area still exist, as do his formal gardens
around the Cortez Palace.

The hunting-lodge is at Alcapancingo, just outside the town; it is
here that Hugh and Yvonne ride in Chapter 4. For Maximilian and
Carlotta this had been their 'Eden'; Lowry seizes on the chances for
symbol-making which this geography and history presents.

Maximilian and Carlotta

Maximilian (1832–67) was the younger brother of the Emperor Franz Joseph of Austria. Tall, attractive and bearded, but rather vain and naive, he was used by the French for their own colonial aspirations and was sent out by Napoleon III as Emperor of Mexico after the civil war of 1859. Maximilian evinced considerable sympathy for the plight of the Mexican Indians within his new Empire. This was far from what had been intended by the French puppet-masters and it became necessary through *agents provocateurs* to betray him to the local revolutionaries led by Juarez. Thus Juarez, a pure-blood Indian, and Maximilian, most liberal of Europeans, were made to fight on opposite sides. Support for Maximilian had collapsed by 1867; he was captured by Juarez and shot.

His young wife Carlotta was spared; she was returned to Europe, where she declined into insanity in the Miramar palace at Trieste. She outlived her husband by sixty full years, not dying until 1927, long, long after the other protagonists in her tragedy were dead and gone. It is assuredly one of the saddest and most haunting stories of modern history.

It is somehow typical that Lowry should have, almost by accident, come to live in the one town in Mexico which could thrust at him this potently symbolic material. He is quick to see the occult links between Maximilian, alienated and abandoned figure of an authority emanating from thousands of miles away, and Geoffrey Firmin, ex-Consul to His Majesty's government, which had totally lost contact with the realities of political life under Cardenas in the late 1930s. And the theme of doom-haunted love with a ruined garden for a setting applies marvellously both to Maximilian and to Geoffrey Firmin, as does the undertow of day-to-day petty espionage and subversion to which both are subjected by hostile and malign agencies.

p.17 – *the barranca*

Right through the town of Cuernavaca, indeed right across Mexico, run a series of ravines. The *barranca* which splits Cuernavaca is used as a symbol by Lowry:

> Quauhnahuac was like the times in this respect, wherever you turned the abyss was waiting for you round the corner. Dormitory for vultures and city Moloch! (p.21)

. . . Ah, the frightful cleft, the eternal horror of opposites . . .
(p.134)

And from the windows of the Farolito it is a sheer drop to the
bottom of this stinking hellish fissure used locally as a rubbish tip.
The Consul himself, like any other mere detritus, is pitched down
the barranca at the end of the novel. Most pictures of the barranca
at Cuernavaca taken in close-up fail to show how extraordinarily
obtrusive it is. Long-distance shots show it like the cleft of the female
sexual organs running, shrub-tufted across the body of the landscape
towards the twin breasts of the volcano peaks. The suggestiveness of
this is not lost on Lowry, and something of the Consul's inability
to find sexual reconciliation comes from his closeness to this pit.
Obviously this symbol of dislocated and destructive nature is related
to and opposed to that of the garden.

p.18 – *the Ferris wheel*
The fairground wheel physically dominates the skyline all day,
reminding us that it is fiesta time. But as an image it does much
more. 'The form of the book . . . is to be considered like that of
a wheel, with 12 spokes, the motion of which is something like
that, conceivably, of time itself' (*SL*, p.67). The book is structured
around twelve chapters, twelve hours, twelve months, so that the
circularity of the thing is complete – it is 7 a.m. when Yvonne
returns, and 7 p.m. when Geoffrey is shot. Even the weather is
cyclic; in Chapter 1 Laruelle is caught by unexpected rain falling
out of season – precisely the same had happened twelve months
before. Lowry expands the meaning of the wheel: 'it is Buddha's
wheel of the law . . . it is eternity, it is the instrument of eternal
recurrence, the eternal return, and it is the form of the book; or
superficially it can be seen simply in an obvious movie sense as
the wheel of time whirling backwards until we have reached the year
before and chapter two . . . (*SL*, pp.70–1). At the end of Chapter 11,
at the moment of her death, Yvonne is aware of the Ferris wheel motif
again, through the wheeling of the stars as she is trodden down by
the horse (p.335).
    One of the novel's most extravagantly comic scenes involves
the Consul mounting the Maquina Infernal (called after Cocteau's
'Machine Infernal') to escape the attention of importunate children
preying on his drunkenness. In this elliptical travesty of a wheel he

is bounced around and turned completely upside down – so that he even sees one of his 'fetish' numbers 666 as 999. But this is more than mere extravaganza and symbol-making. For in the whirling about the Consul loses his passport, and thus abandons his last chance of being correctly identified and spared by the politicos who mistake him for Hugh. Many of the book's symbols have this ability not only to give depth at several pictorial levels, but to forward the story-line at the same time. They are not *merely* decoration.

p.19 – *Parián*

The geography of *Under the Volcano* is atmospherically true to the region in which it is set, but it is far from literally true. Lowry's Parián is a conflation of aspects of Oaxaca and Cuernavaca. The actual Farolito, for instance, is – or was – in Oaxaca. Lowry makes his composite-imaginary town the centre of activity for the local fascists. It is a superannuated place, all its regional authority now leached away to Quauhnahuac, but finding a new identity as home for evil political elements. 'A hell of a place' the good Dr Vigil calls it, with more trenchancy than he is aware of. Lowry himself was adamant: Guanajuato (where Vigil wants to take Geoffrey) equals Life; Parián, Death (*SL*, p.74). 'Years ago there used to be a huge monastery there . . .' recalls Yvonne. 'Some of the shops and even the *cantinas* are part of what were once the monks' quarters.' (p.119)

The Farolito at Parián comprises a series of cell-like rooms each seeming, like a nest of Chinese boxes, to get smaller as one penetrates to their centre. This centre is of course the prostitute María's room, and next door to it is the stinking mingitorio (piss house) – where sits the deformed stool pigeon. The outer cells are occupied by political agitators, while the bar itself is a phantasmagoric ark of cripples, drunks and beggars. All this represents a complete inversion of the building's original function.

p.27 – *the horseman*

The motif of the horseman plays a major part at various levels in the book. The horse in Chapter 1 is a precursor of the one we meet later and also serves to prefigure 'the first appearance of the Consul himself as a symbol of mankind'. Its drunken rider again hints at the Consul, and at mankind out of control – comic and tragic simultaneously (*SL*, p.69).

The horse can represent escape – the mid-morning ride of Hugh

and Yvonne – but this cross-cuts with its meaning as impending
death, for it is on that ride that they first see the Ejidal messenger
riding the horse branded with the number seven. This is the same
equestrian they later find murdered by the roadside. It is the same
horse that Geoff releases as he dies, and which tramples Yvonne.
Thus it weaves in and out of both political and metaphysical
undercurrents to the novel.

p.30 – *Las Manos de Orlac*

Lowry's interest in German Expressionist cinema has been noted
elsewhere. *Las Manos* concerns a concert pianist who, after an
accident, has the hands of a murderer grafted onto his body and
undergoes a complete character change. The tension between the
worlds of creativity and destruction, the debate between free will and
imposed destiny make the subject interesting, although the remake
of the original film – which is the version showing in Quauhnahuac
– is pretty sorry stuff . . . 'Not even Peter Lorre had been able
to salvage it', reflects Jacques Laruelle (p.30). Laruelle himself,
significantly, is a film-maker. His unmade *magnum opus* was to be
a film about Faust! *Las Manos* is originally of German provenance
and this draws in the political strand of the plot. 'For really it was
Germany itself that, in the gruesome degradation of a bad cartoon,
stood over him. – Or was it by some uncomfortable stretch of the
imagination, M. Laruelle himself?', reflects Jacques as he stands
under the poster advertising *Las Manos*. (p.31)

The fact that the same film is on show on the same day two
years running underlines the circularity of time in the novel. Again
this may sound strange, but Lowry records that this is precisely what
used to happen in Cuernavaca in his own days there.

The poster billing this film also takes its place among the random
but pregnant adverts, puffs, and hoardings which flash into and out
of the surface consciousness of the novel. In *Under the Volcano* films,
boxing matches, adverts for insecticide and prophylactic cures for
midge bites all jostle for attention as *montage* on the fringes of consciousness. The technique is, in itself, intensely cinematographic.

There is, of course, a further strand of cross-reference. Both
Lowry's wives had been in films – Jan until an accident left
her scarred, and Margerie until the talkies made inroads into
Hollywood's personnel. It is not surprising to find that Yvonne
(a composite study of the two 'real' wives), should have supported

herself and her drunken father by acting in naive horse operas in Hollywood (cf. Chapter 9 *passim*). And in this we see how the novel's motifs are intertwined circumstantially – the horse-riding and the film symbols overlap deftly and cogently.

Hugh has arrived to visit his elder half-brother, dressed like a '10 cent drugstore cowboy'. He lectures Yvonne (much to her amusement) about equine behaviour, in Chapter 4, and he makes a spectacle of himself – albeit with great aplomb – at the bull-throwing in Chapter 9, where Lowry interweaves flashbacks on Yvonne's youth. But at the same time we gradually realise that his recent holiday ranching on the Mexican border in Texas – playing cowboys, if you will – has brought him in contact with Weber the enigmatic fascist who smuggles Hugh into Mexico. And through this strand of the political plot equestrianism spills across as important to the final destiny of the Consul himself.

p.44 – *The Cabbala*
[The Cabbala comprises the writings which have accreted around the secret traditional lore of Jewish rabbis who read hidden meanings – theological, metaphysical and magical – into the Bible. Most of the specific cabbalistic terms employed by Lowry are glossed below.]

Lowry was interested in the occult, in the supernatural and in the mystical. He had some knowledge of cabbalistic writings – at one time he put himself under the tutelage of a travelling insurance salesman who was, at the same time, a self-acclaimed adept of magical mysteries. Lowry's knowledge was partial, enthusiastic, essentially amateur, but he makes marvellous imaginative use of the Consul's interest in the subject.

> The Cabbala is used for poetical purposes because it represents man's spiritual aspiration. The Tree of Life, which is its emblem, is a kind of complicated ladder with Kether, or Light, at the top and an extremely unpleasant abyss some way above the middle. The Consul's spiritual domain in this regard is probably the Qliphoth, the world of shells and demons, represented by the Tree of Life upside down . . . (*SL*, p.65)

Magic, Faustian, numerological, and Cabbalistic, plays its part in the fabric of *Under the Volcano*.

The sacred book of the Cabbala is the Zohar. This holds that Go
has made manifest His presence in Creation through ten separat
emanations called Sephiroth, which serve as spiritual intermedi
aries between the material world and the invisible. These ar
hierarchically arranged and graphically represented in a schemati
pictorial form called the Sephirotic Tree.[17] Before the fall of Adar
the topmost reaches of this tree were freely available to man, bu
in the post-lapsarian world only the trained adept, possessing th
necessary Cabbalistic secrets, can aspire that high. The topmos
'branches' comprise two groups of three qualities each: right a
the summit are Kether (The Crown); Cochma (Wisdom); Binal
(Understanding). The triad of branches beneath these comprise
Chesed (Mercy); Geburah (Power); Tipheret (Worldly Glory). Eve
this second triad is extremely difficult to attain, and requires chastit
and abstinence on the part of the adept. Violation of the rules
especially wilful violation such as excessive use of alcohol causes th
tree to invert, plunging the lapsed adept into the inverse of heaven
a region called the Qliphoth – 'The realm of husks and demons'.

Of course this notion of inversion projecting a sufferer hellward
also embraces the fairground loop-the-loop, and echoes the shee
perversity of opposites through which the Consul seems physicall
compelled to operate during the day – 'I love hell. I can't wait t
get back there. In fact I'm running. I'm almost back there already
(p.316). And the novel's ending shows the Consul's body thrown int
the barranca.

The theme of the Consul as Faust, and the Faustian tradition c
learning abused and consequent damnation become woven into th
purely Cabbalistic strains of *Under the Volcano*. Geoff is supposed t
be writing a book investigating the boundaries between the norma
and the occult as the books in his library remind us, but his abuse
as an adept, of alcohol, may have taken from him his power to se
into magic, as it has taken away his sexual power.

Throughout those moments of the book where the 'magica
element is stressed we have to read the material of the Cabbala anc
the Faustian echoes as overlapping. Like so many of the symbols i
is first mooted in that all important and contentious first chapter
Sr Bustamente returns to Laruelle a copy of Elizabethan play
which had got mislaid after the Consul had lent it to Jacques
Coincidentally it falls open at Marlowe's *Dr Faustus*, and words lea
off the page at Jacques: 'Then will I headlong run into the earth

Earth gape! O, no, it will not harbour me!' Certainly Geoffrey *does* run headlong to his fate, and in being thrown down the barranca, it might be said that the earth gapes for him. But the identification of Firmin with Faustus is deeper than that. *Faustus* presents a complex statement of the relationship between free will, fate and grace in the mind of a scholar who is cursed with a tragic flaw in the area where conscience and will overlap. The problem for Faustus is that first intellectual curiosity and then moral inertia preclude any search on his part for salvation. There are at least suggestive parallels in the cases of the two ruined scholars.

The link with Elizabethan tragedy is not surprising – indeed, it is material to regard Lowry as positively the most Elizabethan of all modern English novelists. Intellectual curiosity, verbal daring, besotted delight in the curiosity of words themselves, and an uneasy sense of hesitancy about the precise point where man may claim independence of moral authority over his destiny – all these link Lowry to the age of Jonson, Dekker and Shakespeare; these and a positively technicolour sense of daring in the use of symbolism. *Hamlet*, for instance, is stuffed full of image patterns which recur, interweave and cross-fertilise each other, in precisely the same way as in *Under the Volcano*.

p.69 – *the pariah dog*

The book is alive with animals which carry symbolic undertones. Of these the dog is the most important, though goats, scorpions, birds, and cats also play their part in enriching the fabric. The Consul is pursued or haunted throughout the day by pariah dogs. These ultimate outcasts seem to have a natural affinity with him. Their alienation is akin to his own. And when addressed with words of love, these creatures cower and disappear. This happens first at the junction of Chapters 1 and 2, and then again, even more pitiably, in Chapter 7 (pp.231–2). The quality of tenderness which the Consul evinces here is one of the manifold little touches by which we are kept in sympathy with him, despite the wilful and destructive sides of his nature.

It is worth recalling also that in Mexican folklore a dog is killed when its master dies. The belief is that thus the dog may cross the river of death first and swim back to help its owner. Curiously Lowry did not know this until after he had finished *Under the Volcano*, though this in no way invalidates the theme of the Consul being haunted by dogs through his last day, nor the gesture by which 'somebody threw a dead dog after him down the ravine'.

There is also, of course, a structured contrast with the benevolent dog which pursues Yvonne and Hugh on their horse-ride. It is just about the same moment in time when Geoffrey is seeing the snake in his garden that Hugh and Yvonne are being protected from them on their blissful and therapeutic ride to the brewery.

Of the other animals in Lowry's bestiary birds are probably the most potent. Both he and Margerie were keen ornithologists. But again, the birds in the novel are much more than just 'local colour'. Vultures wheel and circle lazily all day as the Consul moves towards his death. Ironically, the driver of the bus carrying them to Tomalín has two doves beneath his shirt – making him a kind of inverted Noah figure; in this he contrasts with the strange old woman in the cantina who keeps a chicken in her bosom. Cervantes, *patron* of the Salón Ofélia, keeps fighting cocks; and just before her death Yvonne releases a captive eagle. Often real birds and delusions from an Hieronymus Bosch world of alcoholic fantasy meld in the Consul's mind:

> Suddenly the Consul thought he saw an enormous rooster flapping before him, clawing and crowing. He raised his hands and it merded on his face . . . (p.372)

and in striking at this phantasm he hits one of the policemen, compounding his already mortally perilous situation.

Scorpions lurk everywhere at the corners of the Consul's vision during that last day – but it is noticeable that he has a covert sympathy with them.

p.87 – *William Blackstone*
Lowry was fascinated by the story of the early American settler Blackstone, which he tells on p.139. Lowry makes trenchant use of parallels between Geoffrey and Blackstone. These only hold good if one takes an indulgent view of the Consul's self-imposed 'living among the Indians', that is, choosing a self-imposed alcoholic retreat, as well as living on in Quauhnahuac after his consulship is terminated – but the self-indulgence helps us to see Geoffrey's tragedy from his own point of view.

And the whimsical fantasy bears terrible fruit at the Farolito.

By this stage the Consul is willing to indulge the irresponsible alias of Blackstone, before the police inquisition. He puts himself in a quite hopeless position, since, to those who want to believe in his guilt anyway he is now either Hugh Firmin – Hugh's telegram is in his jacket pocket – or some spy using Blackstone as an alias. The one fact he cannot prove is that he is Geoffrey Firmin, since both his passport and his will to live have been taken from him.

p.132 – *le Gusta este jardin?*
Literally 'Do you like this garden which is yours? (that is, which is public). Take care not to let your children destroy it.' This is potent enough in terms of the novel's garden imagery elsewhere. But the Consul's mistranslation – 'We evict those whose children destroy it' is even more loaded. Lowry called the sign in the garden 'the most important theme in the book' (*SL*, p.74).

p.199 – *no se puede vivir sin amar*
'It is not possible to live without loving,' from the Spanish poet and religious martyr Frey Luis de León (1528–91). The epigraph obviously applies to the emotional plight of most of the major figures in Lowry's tragedy. The irony is that it was originally written to apply to the love of God for man, not of secular love at all.

INCIDENTAL ICONS

p.23 – *the lighthouse*
A motif with superficially benevolent connotations – lighthouses are agents of comfort and protection; but it is positively inverted through the name – Farolito, 'little lighthouse' – of the evil cantina which, all day, beckons Geoffrey towards death.

Nearly everything Mexican in the novel has an English geographical correlative; the lighthouse, the windmill, the golf course – even local scenery – take on an ability to shift their shapes and to hark back and forth from one world to another. Particularly noticeable in *Under the Volcano* is the evocation of English scenery just before the discovery of the murdered peon in Chapter 8 – and of the parallel evocation of English politics too, through the reference to Mr Chamberlain.

p.23 – *manly carriage*

It is a point of honour with the heavy drinking Taskerson boys
to retain an upright carriage and a sense of dignity, however drunk
they are. The Consul has learned this from them, but a metaphoric
sense overlays the physical in his case. This in turn cross-refers to
the Faustian and Cabbalistic *falling* in the book, and leads to one of
its most delicious comic moments, when Geoffrey falls flat on his
face in the street and has a marvellous encounter with a horribly
English Englishman wearing a Trinity tie but claiming to come
from Caius!

p.38 – *the SS* Samaritan

The name is entirely typical of Lowry's mordant sense of humour.
We are never meant to be quite clear how far Geoffrey was guilty –
at least by default – over the deaths of the U-boat officers captured
by the *Samaritan*. He seems to bear a sense of guilt over it, or is he
merely using it as an excuse? It enables Lowry to develop another
strand in the anti-German theme running through *Under the Volcano*,
but it also demonstrates the crazy brutality which war brings out
in *both* sides. It helps us not to see events in Mexico as merely the
sadistic antics of comic-opera bandits, but as part of the sickness of
the soul which has universally gripped modern man.

p.56 – *the men with dark glasses*

We are never sure of the extent to which the Consul is under
suspicion of being a spy – an espider – even before the arrival of
Hugh. A spooky sense of unsureness follows careful rereading of
the book. At odd moments unexplained young men appear, with
all the trappings of official scrutineers, to be keeping an eye on
the Firmin activities. The reader eventually becomes suspicious of
everybody. Does the bus driver, who is clearly friendly with the
fascists, stop his bus at the Tavern Amor de los Amores to report
in on Geoff and his party. If not, *why* is he described as leaving his
bus and dashing into this place? That Lowry leaves this moment
unexplained seems entirely right. He causes a real jumpiness in a
sensitive reader, and then leaves him to stew in it uncomfortably.
Anyone who has lived under repressive regimes will recognise the
paranoia which ensues.

The role of the inscrutable Weber is equally vague. He is an
out-and-out fascist, probably either a German or an Austrian, and

Hugh was a fool ever to get caught up with him. Presumably he has reported to his Unión Militar pals that he has shipped a commie into Quauhnahuac. Interestingly, Hugh thinks Weber went on to Parián after dropping him off, but we hear his voice in the Bella Vista bar. What is he doing in Quauhnahuac at all? By the evening he has made his way to Parián, where he is drinking as Geoff is tormented and executed. Weber certainly knows that it is a mistake to take Geoffrey for Hugh, but he never lifts a finger to clear up the error.

p.59 – *La Despedida*
The fire-split rock is a powerful icon, representing the rift between Geoff and Yvonne, and, indeed, the split personality of Geoff himself. It implies an unconscious but cosmic sympathy between the state of man and the state of nature in the book, and embraces what Lowry called 'the slow tragic rhythm of Mexico itself'.

A BRIEF NOTE ON MEXICAN HISTORY

Under the Volcano asks us to be aware of pre-conquistador dynastic struggles and regional identities, reminds us of the brutal imposition of European domination on a developed Central American culture, and then swings us into the flux of 'modern' Mexican politics from the mid-nineteenth century forward. This background asks us to see history itself as a series of human tragedies, and without this reading the novel is much weakened.

Herrera and Arista (1848–51 and 1851–3) had attempted to bring quasi-moderate government to a strife-torn country feeling tentatively for a stable sense of national identity. Between 1853 and 1855 came a conservative backlash, offset by 'The Reform' – a liberal countermove led by Alvarez and the pure-blood Indian Juarez in 1855, though, ironically, the indigenous Indian peoples were not an important factor in the reform. Civil war broke out in 1859 and again the Liberals under the military command of Ortega became dominant. This led the French to intervene, ostensibly as peacemakers, really to protect their national assets in the country. They despatched the unfortunate Maximilian and Carlotta as Emperor and Empress of Mexico.

After the deposition of Maximilian another period of chaos

followed, terminated by the heavy and brutal (but effective) hand
of Diaz in 1875. Through to 1911 he ran a middle-class right-wing
dictatorship. This was continued by the next president – Madero –
and led to yet another uprising in the late 1920s and early 1930s.
By 1935 Cardenas had taken power, and he set about a radical
programme of land reform principally through the Ejidal system.
This strove to give small peasant farmers land rights by breaking up
the huge haciendas (ranches) which had been encouraged previously.
Money was lent from a central National Credit Bank to enable small
farmers to till for themselves portions of these vast estates previously
owned by an oligarchic minority. Bank messengers carried cash to
the outlying districts, often at great risk to themselves, since private
armies of desperadoes were encouraged and often paid by the estate
owners to harrass, rob and murder them.

It is often said that Lowry was without political conscience;
he showed little interest in the fashionable left-wing gestures of
his contemporaries at Cambridge. But the plight of Mexico had
clearly moved him deeply by the time he wrote *Under the Volcano*
and it emerges as one of the most powerful political novels of our
time. Its power lies partly in the unpolemical and undidactic nature
of its presentation of events, and, of course, in their inextricable links
with the private destiny of the Consul.

As the novel implies, there was growing German influence in
the country in the late 1930s, making life even more fraught for
an ex-British Consul who is harbouring a half-brother with known
communist sympathies. Of all this Geoffrey is well aware, but he is
long past the stage at which it matters to him, except in so far as he
sees his own life and career as a failure of the individual of goodwill
to withstand arbitrary and arid political systems of any shade.

This strand of the novel reflects fierce arguments which took place
between the ultra-conservative Conrad Aiken and Lowry himself.
The mixed and partly drunken political debate between Geoff and
Hugh in Chapter 10 is very close to real life Aiken/Lowry debates.

It may be worth noting that Lowry's political conscience did
seem to develop in the 1940s and 1950s. The later letters are much
fuller of political discussion than the early ones. In the autumn of
1945 he described himself as 'a conservative Christian Anarchist
. . . (forced to) . . . join the ranks of the petty bourgeoisie'. And
with an entirely typical humour he goes on; 'I feel somewhat like
a Prometheus who became interested in real estate and decided to

buy up his Caucasian ravine' (*SL*, pp.50–51). He writes with typical independence of mind on Russia (*SL*, p.181), on communism and old-fashioned bourgois liberalism (*SL*, pp.211–3) on reactions to the Suez crisis – from an entirely pro-Israeli point of view (*SL*, p.389) – and on civil unrest in Britain (*SL*, p.399). *Ultramarine* is really the only one of his novels in which politics play virtually no part – though even there the antagonism of the sailors to Dana Hilliot is seen partly as a class struggle that is the responsibility of Hilliot to overcome.

Thus the concern with politics in *Under the Volcano* is not really a surprise, especially since the novel grew over a ten-year period during which the war in Europe was taking place, and subsequent to the outcome of the Spanish Civil War. This latter conflict is of some importance to the ideological structure of Lowry's novel, of course, as is the nationalist conflict in China.

4
The Novellas and the Short Stories

'Short fiction was never his forte,' says Douglas Day (p.443). Time and time again Lowry begins with something that looks like a short story but uses it only as a means of expanding his ideas into some other form. There is also an intermediate stage which Lowry called 'novella' – as though this represented a finite and finished genre in itself. But often his novellas represent nothing more than short stories on their way to becoming novels. Apparently on many occasions he did not think about material and predetermine its mould; he simply worked it over and gave it whatever name suited its length at that particular juncture. He nowhere offers a precise definition of what, for him, forms the necessary boundary between short story, novella and novel. Both *Under the Volcano* and *October Ferry* were planned as short stories, and simply grew until they had achieved novel-hood.

Equally symptomatic is the case of 'Elephant and Colosseum', the short story eventually placed fourth in *Hear Us O Lord*. This began as the entry for a sponsored short story competition. The sponsor imposed a limit of 1 000 words, but Lowry's final entry was something like thirty times over the prescribed limit! Material seemed to pour out, and only later to assume a name or a recognisable disciplined genre.

As early as 1950 Lowry had written to James Stern about the problems implicit in working up material for the short story. Here he first mooted the idea of interlinking the individual tales within a collection. This, of course, was a good ten years before he began work on his own major collection.

> ... there is no ... satisfactory design-governing posture for a
> true short-story writer, and I can understand how, difficult to

please as to form, you kick at the amorphousness of the thing
. . . It is possible to compose a satisfactory work of art by the
simple process of writing a series of good short stories, complete
in themselves, with the same characters, interrelated, correlated,
good if held up to the light, watertight if held upside down, but
full of effects and dissonances that are impossible in a short story,
but nevertheless having its purity of form . . . (*SL*, pp.27–8)

Lowry was to return to this notion of interlinked short narratives
some fifteen years later. The publisher's 'note' to his major short
story collection explains that

Lowry had conceived of . . . [*Hear Us O Lord*] . . . as a unit, and
had arranged the tales and short novels of which it consists in
a kind of curve, so that each story had bearing upon those on
either side of it. (*Hear Us O Lord* p.[7])

It is difficult to discern how far this is Lowry's rationalisation – or
at least his own words. The letter to Stern sanctions a belief that
the 'note' reflects the author's intention. Detailed scrutiny blurs
this impression, however. We may identify parts of the curve and
the interlinking dissonances in the version of the collection which
is now published. But the extant letters reveal that the published
collection simply is not the one originally mooted by Lowry.

In October 1951 Lowry confessed quite freely to Matson that he
was using his short stories as practice for the more exciting work of
the full-length novels, and to provide ready-to-hand material which
might induce Erskine to sign a new contract with him (*SL*, p.268).
This letter contains no notion of a pre-determined curve existing
among all or any of this off-the-peg material. Lowry is keen to
sell whatever is saleable. The stories are not all the same as those
eventually collected in *Hear Us O Lord*, and the order is different
from that represented by the published collection.

By May 1952 a positive sense of shape does seem to be emerging
among the short stories. '*Hear Us O Lord* . . . seems to be shaping
up less like an ordinary book of tales than a sort of novel of an
odd aeolian kind itself, i.e. it is more interrelated than it looks
. . .' (*SL*, p.320). This sounds encouraging, except that the mooted
interrelationships are still not between the particular story units
which eventually comprise the published form of the collection. At

this juncture, for instance, *October Ferry* was still intended to be the penultimate story in the volume.

A year later a bulletin of progress to Erskine is still talking about the shape of the collection – but still not the collection we now have. 'The whole thing does have a very beautiful form, and makes a very beautiful sound when taken together,' Lowry declares. *October Ferry* is regarded as a vital part of the organism, yet the same letter later asserts that *October Ferry* must be seen as a novel in its own right – so must 'The Forest Path to the Spring' – but that 'taken in various combinations they form yet further kinds of novel'. These various 'symphonically adjacent companions' seem to be offered as cards to be shuffled and dealt in a bewildering variety of hands. Erskine may even have wondered what game he was supposed to be playing!

None of this finally precludes discussion of *Hear Us O Lord* as a fresh and interesting experiment with the form of interlinked short stories. But it must make us cautious of asserting linkages too dogmatically; it may also explain why the linkages are not all equally strong or convincing within the collection as we have it. It should also be noted that at this time – in the early 1950s – Lowry was talking of twelve 'chapters' for the complete book, not seven, as we now have. Any original concept of shape must have been pulled out of kilter or radically adapted over the years.

Still left in abeyance is the question of the intrinsic artistic merit of the material under discussion, and the value of its final formal disposition; and, even more, the decision in this chapter to discuss the two novellas, *Lunar Caustic* and 'The Forest Path to the Spring' as a pairing, since one of them emanates from the 1930s, while the other was always intended as the conclusion to a group of tales stemming from the 1950s. The *Lunar Caustic* we now have is a splicing and reworking, made in the 1950s, of material from much earlier. It was brought out of storage for further consideration at exactly the same time as the short stories of *Hear Us O Lord* were being composed. Linkages may be stronger than hitherto argued by Lowry's critics. The gain is hopefully of a new perspective on the two works; the ostensible loss is the chance to discuss 'Forest Path' in place as the conclusion of *Hear Us O Lord*. It is hoped that the comments made on it here will still serve to show the logic of its position as the resolution of the short stories.

The work we now call *Lunar Caustic* originated in the period Lowry spent as an inmate in New York's Bellevue Hospital in 1936, during a period of extreme alcoholic depression, following Jan's decision to live apart. Details are vague; exactly how long was the stay in hospital? How voluntary was Lowry's admission there? In any event almost as soon as he left the hospital Lowry felt the urge to write up his experiences. He called his quickly written manuscript 'The Last Address', partly because from his hospital window he could nearly see down to the place where Melville had been living when he finished *Moby Dick*. This first draft of the Bellevue experiences is interlarded with references to Melville, and with variations on the 'great white whale' motif. This or an immediately subsequent draft was actually accepted for publication in *Story* magazine, but an ongoing process of redrafting led Lowry to withdraw the original. It became, almost inevitably, a novella. Meeting with no success from publishers the material was reworked yet again, and given another title – 'Swinging the Maelstrom'. The various versions display substantial tonal differences. In the later version the ending is far more optimistic, and the relationship between patient and doctor is much closer.

A version of this story was given to the French translator of *Under the Volcano* in the late 1940s and eventually published by her, in French, in 1956. Lowry's commitment was stimulated by his; references to *Lunar Caustic* become frequent in the letters, as he took a fresh appraisal of this very old favourite. He attempted to bring together the whole 'bolus' of material from both earlier efforts, but he did not live to complete this task. Like *Dark as the Grave* and *October Ferry* what we have for *Lunar Caustic* is a composite text, edited by Margerie Lowry and others. Despite its vexed publishing history *Lunar Caustic* has always been among Lowry's most popular works.

By reverting to the old 'infernal' material of drunken degradation from the 1930s, and working it alongside the 'paradisal' theme of 'Forest Path', Lowry was certainly creating dissonances, overlaps, and curves of meaning which are consistent with his declared intentions for *Hear Us O Lord*.

The first specific mention of 'Forest Path' in Lowry's published letters comes in mid 1951. He had developed a strongly protective feeling towards the Dollarton shack upon which the novella is centred. Early work upon *October Ferry* brings the comment

Scares of eviction come and go, and it is a situation of some universal significance I have always meant to develop in the novel

. . . the plot of the novel . . . gets into all the short stories too . . .
(*SL*, p.243)

and a little later in the same letter he shows how material spills
over from one project to another as he comments on 'Forest Path':

. . . I have a long short story more or less finished that is out of
the Intermezzo part of the novel – this whole part will be called
Eridanus. This part of the part is known as 'The Forest Path to the
Spring' . . . *Eridanus* is what I call Dollarton here: called such after
the constellation – The River of Youth and the River of Death.
Reading Dante the other day I came to the conclusion that the
celestial scenery of pine trees and mountains inlet and sea here
must be extremely like that in Ravenna, where he died and wrote
. . . the last part of the *Paradiso*. Then I discovered that Eridanus
in mythology . . . *is* the river Po and where the Po emerges to the
sea *is* Ravenna . . . (ibid. p.245)

The very notion of contrast between hell and paradise is consistent
with contrasts to be drawn between *Lunar Caustic* and 'Forest Path'.
   Within a few months the work described in the above letter
had assumed major significance for Lowry. He explained that it
now comprised a novella of great seriousness, which describes the
happiness of his life at Dollarton. It has – and is unique in this
he claims – the kind of seriousness usually reserved for tragedy,
and it deals with human integration. Again the contrast with *Lunar
Caustic*, which is searingly accurate in its discussion of *disintegration*
is very germane.
   The description quoted above sounds, both tonally and themati-
cally, like 'Forest Path' as we now have it. It appears to have been
written much more *currente calamo* than many later Lowry works.
'Forest Path' flows in a reassuring current. Any necessary layering-in
has been skilfully achieved. It conveys a sense of structural integrity
which helps support the work as a lyrical paean of praise, where
both character development and sequential plot are virtually in
abeyance.
   At this date – 2 October 1951 – Lowry could promise that
'Forest Path' should be ready in 'about a month'; this is pretty positive
even for the euphoric Lowry. Two years later the work was still on
the stocks, but whether because it was under revision or because

had become bound up with other material not yet completed, it is difficult to say.

Contrast in the two novellas between purgatory and paradise is manifest enough. Whereas the mid 1930s had been a tormented period for Lowry, the very early 1950s probably represented his most stable and assured period. He was settled at Dollarton, acclaimed as author of a successful novel, domestically at peace, and apparently in control – most of the time – of his alcohol problem. Once he took *Lunar Caustic* from cold storage it is difficult to believe that Lowry would not feel the dynamic contrasts implicit in the two works. Geography, character, ethos, motive, would all point to sharp dichotomies between the two periods. One simple contrastive motif will illustrate the point.

Lunar Caustic describes how, outside the windows of the hospital ward, lies a ruined coal barge, which becomes a focus of attention for the inmates:

> . . . between the two wharves and fast against the poverty grass before the hospital lay the coal barge, sunken, abandoned, open, hull cracked, bollards adrift, tiller smashed, its hold still choked with coal dust, silt, and earth . . . (PMC, p.297)

This passage presents a boat which symbolises destruction, waste, despair. It is in striking and direct contrast with the wrecked freighter in 'Forest Path':

> . . . it had been driven ashore in a wild faen wind decades ago, carrying a cargo of cherries-in-brine, wine and old marble . . .
>
> Gulls slept like doves on its samson posts where grasses were blowing abaft the dead galley, and in early spring pecked their old feathers off to make room for their new shiny plumage like fresh white paint. Swallows and goldfinches swept in and out of the dead fiddley . . . Grass grew too from the downfallen crosstrees, and in the dead winches wildflowers had taken root – wildflowers, spring beauties and death camass with its creamy blooms. (p.226)

The wreck was called *Eridanus* – symbol of both life and death; it gave its name to the paradisal spot where the novella is set, and the passage above is typical of a work which creates a reconciliation between awareness of life and of death. The wreck itself, unlike tha in *Lunar Caustic*, has become an accepted part of an essentially benign disposition. Nature, unimpeded and unvitiated by urban nightmare, has asserted her own benevolent influence upon the potential disaster wrought by man. Thus the one boat, with its coating of grime, detritus, and useless cargo, may represent Lowry's view of himself and of life during the stay in Bellevue (how ironic tha name is, in context!). The boat at Dollarton symbolises a much more reposeful and accepting state of mind. Cherries-in-brine, wine and old marble evoke precisely the opposite feelings to the coal carried on that first wreck.

Taken on its own this contrast might seem forced or fanciful It is possible to show, however, that a series of such contrasts are drawn rigorously and consistently between the two works.

The protagonist of *Lunar Caustic* is a failed musician who has involuntarily allowed his group to disperse, and has now lost al contact with them. In 'Forest Path' the narrator-hero is an ex-jazzband leader who has made his own healthy decision to quit the urban nightlife of his vocation. But he has done so without losing touch with colleagues who still come to visit him. His musical urge has in no way been suppressed, for by the end of the book he has set himself, very successfully, to composing his own works Plantagenet, in *Lunar Caustic*, cannot even play adequately any more Creative life and stultification are thus suggested as the opposing psychic centres of the two protagonists. A list of such oppositions may show just how deeply they permeate these two works when they are considered as a deliberate pairing:

Lunar Caustic	'Forest Path'
Urban, enforced setting	Rural, voluntary setting
Drink dominant and destructive	Drink subsumed into social harmony
Man alienated and isolated	Man at peace with neighbours and environment
A world of lunatic noise	A world of harmonious sound
Blindness or narrowness of outlook	Philosophical and clear-sighted prospect
A world of unavailing doctors	A world of man self-healed

The sordidness of public life	The therapy of private existence
Struggle and suffering for tawdry possessions	Acceptance of Nature's gifts without desire for worldly things
Filthy urban waterway	Self-cleansing Pacific

New York is positively infernal in *Lunar Caustic*. Violent, depraved and unhealthy, the city swelters in the heat wave which becomes a significant aggravation to the hospital inmates, who cannot gain access to the natural elements of cleansing. They are even deprived of basic washing facilities. The river is a murky pathway for commerce and for traffic incomprehensible to the caged-in viewers. They react like animals to movements on its surface:

> Only nightmare ships were left in this stream. All at once, watching the strange traffic upon it, he fancied that the East River was as delirious, as haunted as the minds that brooded over it, it was a mad river . . . where everything was uncompleted while functioning in degeneration. (p.338)

Supporting images drawn from Rimbaud and Baudelaire underline this sense of horror. The contrast with the entirely health-giving spring water of Eridanus is complete and radical. Moreover, where the one is a fixed and arbitrary schemetisation, the other has a quiet fluidity to which man is a voluntary contributing agent. Nothing except paradigms of hell can be drawn from the East River in New York; an entire system of benevolent philosophy can be extrapolated from Eridanus and the associated spring.

It is significant that the narrator of 'Forest Path' has to *learn* by experience to live in accord with the elements; in so doing he ensures his permanent place in the earthly paradise, for the narrator quickly realises that unless he cracks the problem of obtaining a fresh water supply he will be forced back into the city. And whereas the doctors and fellow inmates at Bellevue cannot help Plantagenet to understand or find rapport with the East River, Wilderness's wife and neighbours are active agents in helping him tap the spring.

The handling of the theme of coexistence shows a similar pattern throughout. In Bellevue Plantagenet is surrounded, on the one hand, by those much more genuinely disabled than himself, and on the other by overworked and disheartened medical staff. He struggles to find stasis or rapport with both sides. From among the patients he selects an eighty-year-old displaced Jew and a mentally retarded teenage psychopath. (It is a token of Lowry's skill that he manages to hint that both *may* be misjudged or manipulated by society, but they are 'fixed' by the roles imposed upon them by outside judgement). Kalowsky and Garry are as close as Plantagenet can come to friendship in *Lunar Caustic*. On his other flank is the alternately sympathetic and irritated Doctor Claggart, who regards him as 'an interesting case', but whose sporadic and harassed concern is limited by pressure of time. He is forced to become the agent of authority and of eviction, who has to dismiss Plantagenet and force him back into the external hell of the city.

In 'Forest Path' there is a cognate pattern of characters with whom the protagonist is asked to relate; the local fisherman on the one hand, his wife on the other. Instead of making essentially condescending and ultimately unavailing judgements on his fellow men, as Plantagenet did in Bellevue, Wilderness coexists with his fellow 'inmates' at Eridanus in a marvellously independent but mutually trusting rapport. He has much to learn, and once the trust of the fisherman is won, he is able to complete the learning process, to share, and to give back. His humble recognition of the paucity of his gifts is a major strand in his discovery of sanity and balance. Of all the 'Wilderness' personae present in Lowry's fiction, the one in 'Forest Path' is by far the most complete psychologically, and by far the most congenial. And on his other side stands the therapeutic and genuinely understanding wife who offers support far more comprehensive, meaningful and wise than that which Claggart is able to offer Plantagenet. It is from his wife that Wilderness learns many of the simple but mysterious features of nature and the universe.

Music becomes a correlative of this capacity to learn. In Bellevue the hyperactive negro, Mr Battle, sings a dislocated ballad about the sinking of the *Titanic*. In Eridanus there is communal singing of the hymn which begs protection for mariners against natural disaster at sea – Hear Us O Lord From Heaven Thy Dwelling Place. This hymn accepts that without divine intervention man alone is powerless. It demands humility and offers consolation.

Whereas Plantagenet is driven away from the asylum piano with his music despised, Wilderness has his compositions accepted by the community in which he lives. Beyond the phenomenon of music Lowry contrasts aural stimuli and moods in the two works. 'Forest Path' is full of observation of the minute sounds of nature going about its permanently regenerative and cyclic business; the 'amours of devilfish which sound like cracking machine-gun fire', the low whistle of mating cormorants in the early spring, the swishing wash of boats as they pass, the benevolent noise of Mauger's boatbuilding activities. Conversely, Plantagenet enters Bellevue to the 'dithering crack' of the hospital door closing behind him, and is swamped by a world of cacophony:

> Voices, a prosopopeia of voices, murmured in his ears, ebbed away, murmured again, cackled, shrieked, cajoled; voices pleading with him to stop drinking, to die and be damned ... Music mounted to a screech, subsided. (p.299)

One of the major points of contrast is, of course, the shape which experience gives to the thought of the protagonists. Whereas Wilderness learns, and grows inwardly – he *changes* more than any other Lowry persona – Plantagenet's experiment in self-discovery is totally abortive. Within a few minutes of being cast out from the hospital he is reverting to the habits which first drove him into it. The initial motive forces in the two protagonists are also radically contrasted. Whereas Wilderness has a sensible plan to escape the ruinous life he is leading, but stumbles upon Eridanus by chance, Plantagenet's scheme in entering Bellevue is ill conceived, but quite probably deliberate. More than one commentator has conjectured that Lowry's own admission to the psychiatric ward was a deliberate ploy, like his very descent into the maelstrom of alcohol:

> This plunge into hell, he realised, was what was necessary. He was obsessed with Faust and he sold his soul to the demon drink in order to get a masterpiece. (BBC radio programme, 'The Lighthouse Invites the Storm', 1984)

The closed circle of Plantagenet's world, with the psychiatric ward as its nucleus, reflects this cocoon-like existence, the desire to move in a circle, not to break free. Plantagenet has been circling the hospital for hours before he finally enters. The *movement* of both work and of protagonist in 'Forest Path' is quite different in a dynamically contrastive way.

It is true that Lowry found 'Eridanus' by accident. He and Margerie had intended renting a shack on the Dollarton beach only for a brief honeymoon. If the account in 'Forest Path' is true, their first impressions were anything but paradisal. Yet it rapidly came to represent the only place on earth where he was genuinely happy, and where he could master drink, temper, and paranoia. The saving factor in his almost fetishistic feelings towards Dollarton is that he never lost the recognition that it was a paradise he had worked for, had achieved through spiritual and temperamental self-mastery – and through the hardest physical labour he was asked to give to anything in his entire life.

In reality there were lapses, quarrels, drinking bouts. But none of the frequency, intensity or self-destructiveness of the New York, London, Mexican, or later European phases of his life. Poverty, and distance from a ready supply of liquor undoubtedly contributed, but for most of the Dollarton period Lowry seemed a man not much less contented than the majority of his fellows, and certainly happy with much less than most desired of the world's ostensible 'goods'.

Something of both the battle and the achievement are represented in 'Forest Path'. The sense of balance, of being at one with self and nature, lend dignity to the writing. The prose of this novella is notably tranquil and unconvoluted. It achieves lyricism while avoiding mawkishness. Lowry had no need in this work to strain for characterisation or plot development, and the feel of the piece is genuinely authoritative. It is often said that Lowry could write about nothing but himself. This must be modified; he could write about himself, and Dollarton.

For all its simplicity of outline 'Forest Path' has palpable shape. It gradually assumes spiritual depth and natural understanding until it is able to make these carry an epiphany for its protagonist. It moves through Thoreau-esque celebration of the good and simple life, to achieve a higher dignity. Over the passage of time the narrator grows into harmony with his world. Yet, strategically placed about two-thirds of the way through the narrative, comes a sudden loss of vision and rapport. A massive and inexplicable anger shakes him as he goes about his humble task of carrying water. His equilibrium is destroyed by inability to understand or conquer this feeling:

It was not just ordinary hatred either, it was a virulent and murderous thing that throbbed through all my veins like a passion and even seemed to make my hair stand on end . . . so all-consuming and so absolutely implacable that I was astounded at myself. (p.245)

This breath from the hot furnace of hell intruding into Eden disturbs and disrupts, but it cannot destroy the integrity which has been developed through rapport with nature.

The process of understanding the irrational force springs into focus when Wilderness comes face to face with a mountain lion waiting to spring on him. The creature clearly analogises the hate feeling. It is exorcised by courage and patience. After being stared out and banished by words of charmingly banal conjuration the cougar slinks away. The narrator can return unscathed, but enriched, to his wife and to his way of life, and the story can move onwards to its lyrical conclusion.

Within the novella itself the moment is almost understated. It gains in impact from this undramatic treatment, which serves as a reminder that even in the earthly paradise lurk untamed forces. It shakes any developing sense of complacency. This feeling is supported by the constant emphasis upon physical labour in 'Forest Path' – which again makes it diametrically opposite to *Lunar Caustic*. It is difficult to image any other Lowry protagonist sinking foundations into a rocky foreshore, roofing a dwelling, giving practical help to a boatbuilder. All these skills the intrinsically unhandy narrator has learned for himself, and he is properly proud of his achievement.

It is not the only side of his nature we welcome. Wilderness in 'Forest Path' is the only Lowry persona to make a success of his artistic endeavours. What a refreshing change from the agonised introversion of *Dark as the Grave*, for instance. Perhaps this aspect of the book leans towards wish-fulfilment; the reader, wise after the event, knows that this plateau of balance and stasis will fall away tragically into the rocky barranca of the post-Dollarton years, and thus to messy and tormented death. But as a poem of God's mercy granted through those years of peace on the Burrard Inlet, 'Forest Path' has power, dignity, and coherence. It and the last few chapters of *October Ferry* are the most reposeful writing Lowry ever achieved. They offer a valid alternative to the more widely renowned passion of *Under the Volcano* and to the apparently deliberate contradistinctions made in the contemporary reworking of *Lunar Caustic*. Individually the two novellas offer extreme ends of Lowry's subject matter, style, and personality. Seen as contrastive studies in the problem of human equipoise they have genuine power, validity, and coherence.

The short stories of *Hear Us O Lord* warrant consideration alongside the novels themselves principally because they suggest an experimental interrelationship which asks us to consider them as a unit. As already noted, Lowry mooted to James Stern in 1940 a series of short stories . . . 'complete in themselves but full of effects and dissonances . . . through being interlinked'. During the 1930s Lowry had used the form of the short story comparatively little. He had published six pieces in this genre, but half of these were actually chunks of other works, or the first germs of ideas on their way to full novel-hood. His real burst of energy in the short story came after the 1947–8 trip to Europe. A good deal of the work in the early 1950s dealt with the subconscious tensions between the Old and the New Worlds – not surprising in an author who was so fraught about his own national identity and responsibility. Perhaps the amount of Henry James he had soaked up in his undergraduate days encouraged this interest. The notions of isolation, identity, and yearning homeward are strong in Lowry's writing in the period after 1950.

The interlinkages between the short stories in *Hear Us O Lord* require us to consider the collection as 'another kind of novel' (*SL*, pp.338), though the unscheduled growth of *October Ferry* and other internal changes to the pattern may have blurred whatever shape was originally planned for the collection. The letter to Matson – already cited above, p.79 – is the first time the title *Hear Us O Lord* is mentioned in the published correspondence. The hymn from which it comes was a Lowry favourite:

> There is no hymn like this great hymn sung to the tune of Peel Castle with its booming minor chords in which sounds all the savagery of the sea yet whose words of supplication make less an appeal to, than a poem of God's mercy . . . (PMC, p.223)

Here, perhaps, is the first clue to the manner in which Lowry hoped to achieve his linkages, his 'curve of meaning', in this collection. The hymn itself is a motif in three of the stories. More important, the influence of the sea is felt in virtually all of them alienating, dividing, ultimately annealing. And because there is a note of confidence or hope in many of the stories, we may see how they are unified by a sense of the poetry of God's mercy.

One real problem in considering these stories as an integrated collection may be the difference in quality between them. 'The Bravest Boat' is fearfully mawkish, while the conclusion of the incidentally interesting 'Gin and Goldenrod' is downright silly – no matter what your spiritual tribulations, life will be OK as long as you have hidden a bottle of gin to drink when you get home! These are placed alongside the genuinely interesting and experimental 'Through the Panama', and the considered attempt to link comedy and epiphany in 'Elephant and Colosseum'. Whatever linkages may be intended, the sheer difference in quality of concept and execution is too great here to allow a 'curve' of meaning to emerge with much clarity.

The extent to which the ground plan changed is revealed by the bill of sale for Matson in October 1951. The collection then comprised – and the stipulated order is Lowry's own – 'Through the Panama', 'October Ferry', 'In the Black Hills', 'Strange Comfort Afforded by the Profession', 'Elephant and Colosseum' and 'The Forest Path'. Neither number nor order looks much like the final disposition of material as published. Lowry woos Matson, rather like an importunate door-to-door salesman, 'I could throw in a couple of other short ones . . . ', which scarcely suggests that a tightly organised integrity of outline is yet an exigent part of his planning. Indeed, a version of the work had, by 11 December 1951, been scrutinised by Robert Giroux, Editor in Chief at Harcourt Brace & Co., but his letter (*SL*, p.445) makes it clear the collection is still in 'state One' – that is, comprising the contents and order Lowry had given to Matson above, and might have anything up to 'a dozen or more' added to it.

In January 1952 Lowry declared his desire to finish and publish *Hear Us O Lord* as soon as possible in order to clear the decks for other work, and in the April he offered a confident prediction of completion by 'this fall'. A year later, however, still uncompleted, it has grown to 'twelve chapters', and we have already seen that one segment of it – *October Ferry* – is beginning to get in the way of completion of other projects, to suck in material from elsewhere, and to hover dangerously between being a separate entity and an essential part of the interlinkage in the collection.

The notion of interlinkage is still very strong, however. Lowry comments that 'The whole thing does have a very beautiful form, and makes a very beautiful sound when taken together . . .' (*SL*, p.335). It is now 'less a book of short stories than a kind of novel', but – spare a thought for poor Erskine trying to stave off his superiors' disbelief – Lowry admits in the summer of 1953 that he is now unhappy with the original plan of *Hear Us O Lord* and will need to do some radical rethinking.

Probably the first hint we can take of authorial confidence in the shape we now have for the collection comes from January 1954, when Lowry writes to Matson that the collected stories have begun to take on an interrelated form and to become an independent work of art. There is more confidence in the tone of this letter than heretofore on this subject. Yet our assurance is weakened still by realisation that *October Ferry* is still planned for the penultimate place in this version of the collection.

By now the blow of losing his contact with Erskine had fallen, and Lowry was making plans for his second trip to Europe. Hereafter his work rate dropped off, and never consistently recovered. A brief look at the progress of the individual stories which eventually comprised *Hear Us O Lord* will complete the picture of its uncertain genesis and development.

'The Bravest Boat': written by November 1951 (*SL*, p.269). Published individually in *Partisan Review*, 1954.

'Through the Panama': voyage from which it originated, 7 November to 23 December 1947. Written up at least into a form occupying 60 ms. pages by October 1951 (*SL*, p.267). Probably initially called 'Homage to a Liberty Ship' (Day, p.423). First published posthumously, *Paris Review*, 1960.

'Strange Comfort Afforded by the Profession': idea generated on first European trip, 1948. Intended for *Hear Us O Lord* by 1951. The 'Edgar Allan Poe' material dated from a trip to Haiti as early as 1946. First worked onto the 'Keats' material, summer 1950. First published, *New World Writing*, 1953.

'Elephant and Colosseum': material possibly generated from Lowry's own voyage to the Far East, late 1920s. Then from his 1948 visit to Rome. Entered for short-story competition, late 1951. Listed as item 5 for *Hear Us O Lord* in October 1951. Ms. specified as '100 pages', but still being worked over as a 'short novel', November 1953 (*SL*, p.347). First published in *Hear Us O Lord*, 1961.

'The Present Estate of Pompeii': generated from the 1948 trip to Europe. 'Nearly finished', November 1950. First published, *Partisan Review*, 1959.

'Gin and Goldenrod': 'Not so nearly finished', November 1950 (*SL*, p.216). Genesis may have been in an episode recorded by Day (p.302), which occurred during the Lowrys' stay in Niagara-on-the-Lake late 1944. First published in *Hear Us O Lord*, 1961, where it lies uneasily in the slot once intended for *October Ferry*.

'The Forest Path to the Spring': generated out of personal experience during the earlier Dollarton years. First mentioned in *SL*, June 1951. Promised to Matson for November 1951, as containing about 100 pages. First published in *Hear Us O Lord*.

At one stage another story, entitled 'Ghostkeeper', was intended for inclusion. Day records it as follows: '. . . another of his writer-being-written-about pieces, it was abandoned after he had written only a few pages . . .' (Day, p.431). Mention of this abortive fragment offers a further clue at least to intended linkages across the curve of the collection. The setting for 'Ghostkeeper' was to have been Stanley Park, Vancouver, where 'The Bravest Boat' is also set.

These, then, are the facts from which we have to extrapolate the artistic design and intention for the finally published collection. They do not suggest a consistent dynamic shaping energy. A shape does emerge, but its outline is affected by the various vicissitudes which befell the collection over the years.

There is another major problem, concerning a lack of consistency in the central persona. The protagonist of 'The Bravest Boat' never reappears; in 'Through the Panama' the narrator is a deliberately whimsical *mélange* of pseudo-author, 'real' author, and fictive character, Sigbjørn Wilderness – the 'real' author above – reappears in the third story, but is replaced by Kennish Cosnahan in the fourth. 'The Present Estate of Pompeii' uses Roderick Fairhaven as protagonist; Wilderness comes back in the sixth tale, and the narrator is anonymous, though implicitly Wilderness again, in 'The Forest Path'. This situation is compounded when we find Lowry telling us that even Wilderness is not to be regarded as a consistent entity; he represents various aspects of the protean character of Lowry himself.

It is essential, therefore, to rid ourselves of the urge to seek consistency of outline through *character* as such. The continuum of the work is found at a more obscure level of psychic development. Fragments of personality – indeed *aspects* of a central neurosis – hold the stories into a curve of meaning. The apparent assurance in the first story breaks down in 'Through the Panama' to such an extent that the author is in search of an author who is in search of a character. The middle stories examine further isolated aspects of a central social nervousness and inability to integrate. And the final triumphant narrative shows the author-figure at last in an aspect of repose. A number of themes are developed around this idea of the central characters' search for equipoise.

Mawkish as it is, 'The Bravest Boat' introduces several motifs which will be sustained and built up as the collection of stories unfolds. Against the peri-urban and maritime setting of a Canadian municipal park two lovers meditate on endurance, constancy and spiritual stability. Most of the material in the later stories harks back to these points. Sigurd and Astrid have been brought together through the agency of a toy boat to which, as a boy, Sigurd had committed a message. For twelve years the tiny craft wandered the ocean, surviving storm and calm, until Astrid found it, contacted Sigurd, and became his wife. The story fails because of technical deficiencies, particularly in the exquisitely awful dialogue. Astrid's share of this comprises virtually nothing but repetition of Sigurd's not very strong lines, to the point where the reader is convinced that she must be half-witted. The *idea* of the story is admirable as a lyrical introit to material which will be explored later (fortitude, triumph over adversity, harmony with nature); its execution is very weak.

The contrast with 'Through the Panama' is well conceived as an idea. Sigbjørn Wilderness and his wife Primrose are journeying from Canada, down the Pacific coast to the Panama Canal, then into the Caribbean and, via Curaçao, across the Atlantic to France. This is, of course, the trip which Malcolm and Margerie undertook 1947–8. Almost inevitably the protagonist is haunted by his projected next work – a novel about Martin Trumbaugh, a novelist who has written and been haunted by a novel he wrote about Mexico. The weird *mélange* of personae enables Lowry to create a good deal of comic introspection about the nature of identity, and about personal equipoise. 'How can the soul take this kind of battering and survive? It's a bit like the toy boat,' exclaims Martin, after a particularly hefty spasm of self-doubt – almost as though he had been occultly connected with 'The Bravest Boat' itself. Later, out in the Atlantic and heading for the new trials of Europe as a spiritual testing ground, the SS *Diderot* will be battered almost as the toy boat was in the earlier tale. Through shedding care for self and being purged by the proximity of death in the storm, it is implied that the narrator may emerge as a better integrated and more understanding man.

For most of the duration of the story we are given a marginal gloss, in the manner of that provided by Coleridge for 'The Ancient Mariner', and this enables Lowry to extract further parallelisms and overlaps in the ideas-fabric of his work. Wilderness's albatross is, presumably, his social diffidence and his spiritual confusion. The vultures seen off the coast of Mexico evoke a specially potent cross-reference to the traumas previously experienced there, and the entire nexus of neurotic hang-ups is syphoned through the Panama Canal, and then purged by the near-fatal storm in the Atlantic.

The last of the marginal glosses reads:

> And the Ancient Mariner beholdeth his native country.
> And to teach by his own example, love and reverence to all things that God made and loveth. (PMC, p.98)

For all this solemnity 'Through the Panama' is often very funny. This aspect of the story saves it from morbidity and self-pity. Yet at bottom the bravura essay represents a touchingly serious attempt to move through the fear and pity implicit in the prayer 'Hear Us, O Lord' towards an ultimate reconciliation of a haunted man with his causes of terror. Embedded in its maritime/mariner/fraught soul themes there is a subterranean linkage back towards a central core of ideas within the volume as a whole.

'Through the Panama' is an inventive fantasia – one of the most original pieces of travel writing of this century. But its real travel is inwards into the haunted consciousness of its protagonist. The correlations between inner and outer states sometimes become too heavily portentous – particularly in the description of the god-like Authority figure who controls the canal locks. The work is also capable, however, of parcelling up some of Lowry's most genuine notions on character, the novel, criticism. It manages to strike a balance between clownishness and high seriousness which is rare in his writing outside *Under the Volcano*. Aspects of the inward-looking investigation, and the attribution of correlatives of despair to inanimate objects makes 'Through the Panama' closely akin also to *Lunar Caustic*. Its calculatedly eccentric manner of presentation is initially daunting, perhaps, but once this is penetrated it justifies itself, and the story stands as one of the most satisfactory and completed things written by Lowry. The difference in intention and in execution between 'The Bravest Boat' and 'Through the Panama' is very large. Thus for all the arguments urging that they are progressive parts of any curve of meaning, there remains an implicit disjunction between them.

In 'Strange Comfort Afforded by the Profession' Wilderness – here minus his wife – has arrived in Rome on a Guggenheim fellowship (Lowry had at one time hoped for such an award himself, but it never materialised). Wilderness is dislocated and thrown off balance by the intrinsic strangeness of the Old World; this Jamesian motif runs right through the 'Roman' section of the collection. In a sense it is implied that even the storm and cleansing of 'Through the Panama' has been at best partial. The protagonists of 'Strange Comfort', of 'Present Estate' and of 'Elephant and Colosseum' all share this feeling of cultural and social apartness. After his years of self-imposed isolation it would be strange had not Lowry himself felt this when he made his return to Europe.

The story of 'Strange Comfort' pursues the curious sense of affinity felt by Wilderness with the tragic literary and historical figures who have suffered, died, and been memorialised in Rome. He notes down phrases from the Keats and Shelley Museum as they appear to cross-refer to his own artistic *Angst*, and these become mixed in his notebook with details of the suffering of the early Christians and victims of Roman oppression. Subsidiary characterising touches reveal Wilderness as homesick, incompetent, and bewildered by the Eternal City's noise and bustle. This helps to relieve the 'arty' introspections of the story.

The 'strange comfort' of the title is, by implication, a mixture of the fellow creator's pride, together with relief about his (so far) capacity to survive crises which have annihilated fellow artists. There is a concessive touch of humour in juxtaposing the little private neuroses of Wilderness with the harrowing letters and memorials of Keats' death struggle as manifest in the museum showcases.

The narrative is enriched by Sigbjørn's discovery of the notes of a not dissimilar visit he had previously paid to the Poe memorial in Richmond, Virginia. While there he had recorded the agonised pleas

Poe had made to his foster-father for support – 'for God's sake pity me and save me from destruction'.

This in turn is paralleled and overlaid by the discovery of a similar letter which Sigbjørn himself had written in appeal to the Los Angeles lawyer who had charge of his affairs at the nadir of his fortunes. The themes of the struggling artist, the world's indifference, the uncaringness of Authority, and the preservation of an inner balance are thus conveyed in layers of experience set on top of each other. Those who know the Lowry biography will recognise that the author has attributed, almost verbatim, to Wilderness, a letter which had been written to his lawyer when Malcolm Lowry was first evicted from Mexico. Through the persona of Wilderness he is able to link fact and fiction, history and biography, personal and public torments. However obliquely, he is also able to stitch 'Strange Comfort' onto 'Through the Panama', with its handling of storm, disruption and strange comfort. The repeated plea 'For God's sake pity me' is a variation on the leitmotif 'Hear Us O Lord'. The story is an incidental rather than a central document. It lacks the excitement which its experimental dynamics give to 'Through the Panama'. But 'Strange Comfort' offers a cogent and unusually well-balanced account of some of the Lowry shibboleths and nightmares.

'Elephant and Colosseum' offers another Roman epiphany, this time in comic form. Kennish Drumgold Cosnahan, like Wilderness before him, is meditating in a Roman bar upon, *inter alia*, his incompetence in practical matters, his artistic obscurity, and his sense of loneliness in enforced isolation from his wife who has had to remain behind in the New World. The ocean divides two radically different cultures which share only the bewildering common ground of an identical language. Yet since he is in Italy – and speaks virtually no Italian – even his English is of scant use to him. The 'tower of Babel' motif is underlined by the fact that Cosnahan (who keeps breaking into Manx speech) is in Rome to check up on the non-appearance of the Italian translation of his novel, 'Ark to Singapore'. This work, based on Drumgold's experience as involuntary minder of an elephant on a sea voyage from the Far East, has had a brief but flashy success in America, but none in the Old World.

Drumgold himself is caught uneasily between the two. His mother was a Manx white witch, and his brothers respectively a Catholic priest on that intensely non-conformist island, and a liberal anarchist

recently unsuccessful in a *coup d'état* against the government of S
Helena! Whimsical humour in abundance is woven out of thes
confused strands, though all clearly enough bear back upon th
identity and confidence problems in Cosnahan himself.

After a comically unsuccessful attempt to trace his publisher
(who are in Turin, not here in Rome at all), he wanders into th
zoo and encounters the very elephant which he had nursed throug
a storm in the China Sea many years ago. The unexpected joy o
this reunion establishes a new confidence and balance in him, an
he is aware that his impetus to work has magically returned.

Here Lowry has taken a stage further the motifs present i
'Strange Comfort'. On a literal level the 'comfort' in 'Elephan
and Colosseum' is even stranger, but more positive and tangible
The artist is preparing for a healthy future rather than bolsterin
himself by drawing analogies with a morbid past. The unlikel
agent of metamorphosis is the elephant, Rosemary, who – like th
bravest boat – and like the protagonist of 'Through the Panama
has survived her own *Storm und Drang* and emerged as a strang
comfort to others.

The story is too long and tries to cram in too many ancillar
themes, but it weaves some delightfully comic parabolas aroun
the character of the bewildered Cosnahan, who is one of Lowry'
most likeable personae. The quality of the experience at the meetin
between Cosnahan and Rosemary is nicely redolent with bot
sentimentality and balancing humour.

Up to this point in the volume the links between the storie
on an implied curve have been discernible without forcing th
material, and seem to justify Lowry's claims about the novelty of th
collection as an interlinking nexus of stories and ideas. The next tw
units seem not only among the weakest in themselves, but also th
most feeble links in the chain. 'The Present Estate of Pompeii' ha
New World schoolmaster Roderick Fairhaven behaving churlishl
on a trip to Pompeii made for his wife's gratification. He refuse
to be excited by the ruins of the ancient city. Once cajoled ou
of the bar and onto a guided tour he insists on counterpointin
his iconoclastic interjections against the broken commentary o
Signor Sallaci, the appropriately named Italian guide. The clash
of Old and New Worlds is shadowly present through Fairhaven'
hankering for the freshness of Eridanus as opposed to the sleaz
timeless prurience of Pompeii, and a life/death schism is represente

by the contrasted locations. Perhaps it can be argued that we are beginning now to slip down the curve which will carry us, two stories later, back to the Burrard Inlet. Some of Fairhaven's *sotto voce* observations on the culture schism are apposite enough: ' "In Germany, England, red light" ' . . . says Sr Sallaci, doing his guided tour of Pompeiian brothels . . . ' "Roman better idea. Cock outside." Well, St. Malo was wiped out, Naples defaced, but a cock in the street outside a Pompeiian brothel still survived. Well, why not?' Fairhaven can throw off such whimsical *obiter dicta* which are amusing enough, but neither he nor the story itself gathers sufficient momentum to warrant much attention. The piece is ephemeral and inconsequential, a verso page from Lowry's travel notebook. Its roots are too feeble to penetrate far into the soil of the design-governing posture of *Hear Us O Lord*.

The penultimate place in the collection caused major problems once *October Ferry* outgrew its role. 'Gin and Goldenrod' simply cannot fill the gap; it has little architectonic rationale within the overall curve of the book. Nor does it have the saving graces of sly humour and trenchant observation which save much of the 'Roman' part of the collection. This story returns to the kind of earnest but uncritical self-consciousness which caused unwitting archness of tone in 'The Bravest Boat'.

In 'Gin and Goldenrod' Wilderness has been forced into a penetential return visit to the sleazy house of a bootlegger where he had been on an expensive bender the previous Sunday. Here he had incurred both debt and social opprobrium. Now, accompanied by the long-suffering Primrose, he painfully retraces his steps through the desolation of abomination caused by the speculative builders who are raping the forestland around his home. We are meant to realise that through this scenery he recognises with shame and chagrin the metaphorical desolation which his alcoholism causes in his domestic life, and how this is reduplicated in the ecological theme of the ruination caused by mindless and greedy progress impinging upon the forest paradise. But the story is an intrusion upon the larger themes sounded around it. Well enough observed and written with some vigour, it evokes incidental feelings of environmental horror in which the reader may well wish to share. The problem is really in the utter feebleness of its conclusion and, such as it is, the wrongness of that conclusion at this stage on the implied curve towards purification and regeneration. Sigbjørn pays his sordid debt to the bootlegger and he and Primrose make the return journey in a more hopeful spirit, which is symbolised by the capacity of the wild flowers to survive even in the developers' wilderness. The voyage home, too, is, albeit thinly, populated with more benign figures in the landscape than the outward trip. So far so good, but the conclusion is purely bathetic:

'I have a confession to make Sigbjørn' . . . (Primrose) . . . said . . . 'You didn't lose that bottle of gin. You gave it to me when you came back the next morning. But I put it away and then you thought you'd lost it.'
'Then we can have it now.'
'Sure. And we can have a cocktail when we get back.'
'Good girl.'
They stepped into their own woods and the cat came leaping to meet them. In the cool silver rainy twilight of the forest a kind of hope began to bloom again. (p.215)

It is easy to see why *October Ferry* was originally intended for this moment on the curve, when 'hope began to bloom again'. In *October Ferry* this is precisely what does happen, and we are given plenty of supporting evidence as to how and why this should be so. The hope itself is a legitimate one and is validated by events in the story. But why or what the hope relates to in 'Gin and Goldenrod' must remain problematic. Nearly all Lowry's personae in *Hear Us O Lord* are drink ridden, and striving to fight it. This particular sense of progression across a curve is quite strong from 'Through the Panama' onwards. The point is that drink becomes increasingly a conquerable entity. But in 'Gin and Goldenrod' all the implications are that the earlier traumatic experience has gone for nothing. Wilderness will soon be back at his old vice – sanctioned by Primrose. If for no other reason, the story is out of place here.

Nor can it bear the burden of carrying us into the lyrical repose of 'The Forest Path'. In 'Through the Panama' Wilderness had noted that he strove to 'turn this into triumph; the furies into mercies'. In 'Forest Path' this transmutation is achieved. *Hear Us O Lord* began with the lovers brought together by the magical sea change of 'The Bravest Boat', and it ends here where spring and sea water naturally merge on the Eridanus foreshore. Implied is the reconciliation of all the tensions which informed the voyage out and the European visit. In 'The Bravest Boat' caged cougars symbolise the manic and destructively cramped fury of nature on which urban impulses have set a cruel constraint. In 'The Forest Path' the cougar is free and passes by the vulnerable human who meets it on the path. They achieve a moment of stasis if not of rapport. The birds in 'Through the Panama' and the beast in 'Elephant and Colosseum' help pencil in this dimension to the curve arcing through the book. And in the repose and harmony which 'The Forest Path' achieves one can finally sense the purpose and the achievement of these stories as an integrated entity. It is a brave and valid experiment, vitiated in part by disruptions to the plan as work progressed, and dislocated by poor quality of both concept and execution in places. But without this collection in its attempt at a strange and new kind of unity, the Lowry canon would certainly be impoverished.

5

The Posthumous Novels

It has become a commonplace of Lowry criticism that his two last novels show an attenuation of passion and a significant falling-off in achievement from the tragic intensity of *Under the Volcano*. There can be little doubt of the general truth of this. Had he never written his one recognised masterpiece it is unlikely that he would be remembered as an important novelist on the strength of either *Dark as the Grave* or *October Ferry*. This general assumption may, however, conceal the integral differences in kind and intention between the two posthumous novels themselves. Whereas *Dark as the Grave* is a studied exercise in a kind of literary parasitism, *October Ferry* seems to be tentatively striking out into new territory. Its hero is the only Lowry protagonist to have – or to have had – a regular profession; he is the only one to have children; and he is the only one whose spiritual recovery at the end of the book seems remotely assured. Technically *October Ferry* may be the least finished of all the novels. Its chapters are much shorter – on the page no other Lowry novel even looks like this. Its internal coherences through the overlaying of circumstantial icons are less complete. It is avowedly the most middle class in its social aspirations. All Lowry's other heroes are natural rebels or outsiders; Ethan Llewellyn is struggling desperately to achieve, or rediscover, social integration. Much of this looks intentional, but some may be due to incompleteness of the book at the time of Lowry's death. But manifestly *October Ferry* is seeking a new gentleness of soul in its protagonist. Contrasts between the two posthumous novels are far more germane than superficial likenesses implicit in authorial incompleteness.

The process of composition in *Dark as the Grave* is the familiar one of slowly attempting to distil personal experience and to shape it by layering in icons and symbols which will help to make the experience

102

bear a significance beyond itself. This process was brought to finality by Lowry himself with neither *Dark as the Grave* nor *October Ferry*. He dashed from one project to another, leaving both at times to chase other hares through film scripts and the short stories. Also at this time, in the early 1950s, his work schedule was disrupted by trips abroad. Finally he abandoned the incompleted *Dark as the Grave* in a bank vault – though sporadic work went on with *October Ferry* virtually until his death. All these factors leave the posthumous work without a honed-up cutting edge. There are plenty of critical voices which simply declare that Lowry had run out of steam. Cause and effect are confused over those last blurred years. It is certainly difficult to fault the publishers who lost faith in Lowry and cast him adrift, though this lack of confidence may in itself have contributed to his breakdown as a consistent creative artist.

Like virtually everything he wrote, *Dark as the Grave* is based upon events which actually befell Lowry himself. On 7 June 1944 his shack at Dollarton was burned to the ground. The manuscript of *Under the Volcano* was rescued, but *In Ballast to the White Sea* was almost totally consumed. The trauma of losing his beloved dwelling was enormous, and the psychic disturbance took years to settle, even superficially. Hereafter fire was to be added to the list of fetishes capable of causing absolute panic in Lowry's mind.

Threats of eviction from Dollarton had also become more frequent and more intense; with *Under the Volcano* still not quite finished, no home, and an uncertain future, his state of mind was deplorable. A letter to Conrad Aiken (*SL*, pp.47–52) describes the ongoing as well as the immediate effects. We shall find them again, thinly fictionalised, in *October Ferry*.

With Margerie clutching *Under the Volcano* in her luggage, the Lowry's abandoned the fire-scarred wreckage of Shack 2 in July 1944, to stay with friends in Ontario. The novel was finished – at least the manuscript was finally wrested from Lowry – on Christmas Eve. The couple had now recovered enough to face the wreckage of their home on the Burrard Inlet, and they began the process of rebuilding. Later that year it became clear that renovations would not be complete in time to offer adequate protection from the Vancouver winter. By now the manuscript of *Under the Volcano* was on its travels – yet again – around the publishers on both sides of the Atlantic, and with money in hand from the settlement of Lowry's father's estate,[18] they decided to take a holiday. Margerie was eager to see all the places mentioned in the novel she had spent years typing and retyping. And Malcolm had lost touch with the rather mysterious but charismatic 'Juan Cerillo', who had figured in *Under the Volcano* as Dr Vigil, and who had been spiritual mentor and boozing buddy in Lowry's earlier Mexican years. Letters to Cerillo had been returned unopened, and he had begun to assume a fetishistic significance.

Leaving instructions that any correspondence about *Under the Volcano* should be forwarded, since Jonathan Cape had sent a provisionally encouraging letter about it, Malcolm and Margerie left Canada on 28 November 1945, for Mexico City. By the end of the year they were settled in Cuernavaca, and Lowry was beginning to soak up the atmosphere of the Paradisal/Infernal settings of his novel. Added to his neuroses was the recent appearance of Charles Jackson's book, *The Lost Weekend*.[19] This story of drunken amnesia and squalor elicited strong feelings of frustration and chagrin in Lowry. He had begun his drink-oriented novel long before Jackson, but both story and film of Jackson's account rather trumped Lowry's ace, so he felt. The old fear of accusations of plagiarism came back, along with frustration that his effort would be misjudged as repetitive. In truth *Under the Volcano* was both more intense and more original than *The Lost Weekend*, but Lowry can be forgiven for not seeing this at the time.

On New Year's Eve 1946, when Lowry was sliding into a serious alcoholic torpor, induced by his sense of being haunted by events and places from the past, came a letter from Cape. The London publisher wrote that, although he was impressed by *Under the Volcano* he felt considerable rewriting was essential before it could be published. Fighting off the utter frustration that ten years of writing and redrafting had still not achieved success, Lowry set about writing to Cape the now famous letter in which, chapter by chapter, he justified the book as it stood (*SL*, pp.57–88).

In the middle of this herculean and frustrating task, itself vitiated by moods of despair, heavy drinking, and domestic tension, Lowry made a suicide attempt on the night of 10 January, when he attempted to slash his wrists. Despite this – perhaps in expiation for it – he pulled himself together enough to take Margerie down to Oaxaca on 16 January in pursuit of the missing Juan Cerillo. Since Oaxaca had been the City of Dreadful Night in the bad days when Jan abandoned him in 1936, this trip made further inroads into Lowry's resilience. There had already been strange coincidences to assault and disturb; on arrival at Cuernavaca the Lowrys found accommodation by chance in precisely the building which had been the setting for Laruelle's studio in *Under the Volcano*. Faces and events from the past leaped out to haunt and taunt. If Cerillo had been Lowry's self-appointed good angel there had been a corresponding shadowy figure (called Bousfield) who had somehow been associated with humiliation and degradation, and whose presence Lowry now feared as much as he longed for Cerillo. For a man so volatile, unstable, and sensitive to coincidence the whole trip may seem curiously ill advised. Yet on one level a curious kind of peace seems to have emerged.

Enquiry in Oaxaca proved that the unfortunate Juan Cerillo was dead, and had been for some years. He had been shot, while drunk, in a tavern brawl. Other spectres from the past were similarly emasculated or laid to rest. The original 'Farolito' – scene of the Consul's death – was closed; the Salón Ofélia had become a drugstore; the evil angel, Bousfield, turned out to be no more than an elderly and lecherous roué when Lowry came face to face with him. The town of ghosts was now merely a ghost town.

The trip still had a tragi-comic twist. In early March, while visiting Acapulco, shortly before they were due to head back to Canada, the Lowrys fell foul of the Mexican immigration authorities. Weeks of delay followed, in which they were subjected to cheating, prevarication and frustration. They could not leave . . . they could not stay; they were to be deported . . . they were to be imprisoned. Even the arrival, early in April, of simultaneous letters from Cape and Reynal confirming that *Under the Volcano* was accepted, uncut and unaltered, seemed virtually irrelevant in the midst of this authoritarian baiting. Finally, on 4 May, they were bundled across the border at Nuevo Laredo. The most detailed account of this encounter with malign authority is the sworn statement made by Lowry to a Californian lawyer (*SL*, pp.91–112).

The Lowrys were back from their Mexican trip by June 1946, and were soon occupied proofreading *Under the Volcano*. Late that year and early into 1947 they were away in Haiti, celebrating the imminent appearance of the book. Lowry's letters reveal that he was working on more Mexican material. *La Mordida*, intended to describe the immigration fracas was under way by the spring of 1947 (*SL*, p.141), and by 13 August of that year Lowry declared that he had written 'the first of a first draft of *Dark as the Grave* (*SL*, p.151).

In October a letter to Albert Erskine states '. . . I am writing what fairly can be described as a good book – I'm not sure, of course, precisely, being a kind of sidestreet to my own consciousness; . . . We progress towards equilibrium this time instead of in the opposite direction . . .' (*SL*, p.157).

This seems to refer to early stages of *Dark as the Grave*. If so, it has already taken over from the embryonic *La Mordida* which had been front runner among Lowry's work in progress six months earlier. Such shifts of loyalty among his projects, and attempts to hold many projects in hand concurrently become more and more frequently – and alarmingly – symptomatic of Lowry after 1947. Neither *Under the Volcano* nor *Ultramarine* came out of self-induced chaos of this kind. The numinous grand schema for *The Voyage that Never Ends*[20] may have been invented partly as excuse for this developing habit of trying to work on everything at once.

It is March 1949 before the published letters again mention the 'new book' – still conjecturally *Dark as the Grave*. Quite a lot of 1948 was side-tracked into an epic script-cum-exegesis of *Tender is the Night*; anything rather than complete the task in hand, perhaps. In that March letter to Erskine, the agent is informed that the new book is 'like a dark belittered woodshed I'm trying to find a way around in with a poor flashlight'. By July it is absorbing him up to fifteen hours a day (*SL*, pp.173 and 180). Presumably Lowry is trying to compensate in advance for the long hiatus caused by the trip to Europe (November 1947–January 1949), during which little serious writing was done. It is interesting that he chose *Dark as the Grave* not *La Mordida* to take with him on that journey, at least in the pious hope of doing some work. Yet letters from later dates will still occasionally revert to discussing *La Mordida* as the favoured project.

It is in October 1951 that Lowry declares that the new book is 'tentatively' called *Dark as the Grave*; it is a 'sort of Under Under the Volcano, ten times more terrible . . .' But it is clear from this same letter that a good deal of creative energy has been hived off simultaneously into at least half a dozen major short stories, and into the commencement of *October Ferry* as a novella. Poor Erskine, waiting for coherent news of the outcome of Lowry's long-term contract with his publishers, then gets informed on Ash Wednesday 1952 that '*Dark as the Grave*, *Eridanus* and *La Mordida* are together a trilogy and though they might well be published separately . . . I can't *think* of them at present separately.' The same letter (*SL*, pp.304–9)

also makes us aware that the short story collection *Hear Us O Lord*
has taken up a good deal of time, and, God help Erskine, that the
novella *Lunar Caustic*, drafted in the 1930s and again in 1940, has
been reinstated among the important works in progress. *Dark as the
Grave*, Lowry conjectures, might be completed, amidst all this other
work, in a further two years' time. Then, suddenly in August 1952,
he announces that '*Dark as the Grave* – 700 pages of notes and drafts
is deposited in the bank . . .' (*SL*, p.322).

And there, as we can see from Douglas Day's Preface to the
novel, it sat until 1965, in the inchoate form of three separate
drafts. It had been banked by Lowry just as the new favourite,
October Ferry, began to elbow its way forward. And presumably the
loss of his ongoing contract with Reynal in January 1954 made it the
more daunting to pull back from storage for yet further patching and
superimposing, something which had in the past proved intractable.
The presumption is that Lowry never again so much as looked over
the material he had assembled for *Dark as the Grave*.

The plot concerns a novelist who has written an unaccepted
book about Mexico, which he is now visiting with his second
wife. They drink, quarrel, relive the past. And the old friend
whom they have come south to seek is discovered to be dead.
This plot is manifestly an account of the Lowrys' own trip. It
is much closer to reality, detail to detail, than that of *Under
the Volcano*. Thus there is an immediate critical question to be
asked about the reworking of fact into valid fiction. Events which
make sense within the world of the private individual may not be
capable of taking on a large enough significance to warrant their
appearance within the framework of fiction. More importantly,
the fictive account requires a process of selection and a conclusion which validates the experience and gives it final shape.
But real life tends not to produce such moments; distancing,
revalidating, shaping.

The structure of Lowry's novel is characterised by typical tangents,
insets and accretions of meaning. But, compared with the work in
Under the Volcano, the later book reveals few signs of being subjected
to radical organisation of material which might manifest a higher
purpose or cosmic irony. It takes the book a quarter of its twelve
chapters even to get us to Mexico. The journey down is, typically,
littered with retrospects, flashbacks and the evocation of personal
shibboleths. These are often too small and too personal to be capable

of development into aspects of the life of a protagonist who might command respect or interest. Far too much of the time Sigbjørn Wilderness comes across merely as silly, selfish, flabby minded Furthermore, despite the claims made in Douglas Day's Preface there is no sign of the strand of wit which so helps to strengthen *Under the Volcano*. The verbal parabolas in *Dark as the Grave* are faddish rather than dynamic, and at no stage does the novel create situational humour to compare with at least half a dozen episodes from the earlier novel.

The lack of sinew in both style and character may be fairly illustrated by the following:

> A scene that had taken place just this morning at the Vancouver airport came back to him vividly. When their airliner limousine had drawn in at the airport entrance, a police car had been standing in the rain outside, and possibly it was this that had put him off. Sigbjørn had fumbled and dropped his tickets, forgotten to give one bag in to be weighed, and become covered with confusion, and it was not until Primrose and he were seated finally on a bench waiting for the southern flight to be called that it occurred to him that the presence of the police car was probably a matter of course . . . With this realisation Sigbjørn sighed with relief and was able to give himself for a while wholly to Primrose and their excitement. Meantime they had watched, through the French windows of the waiting room, a big plane arriving from Seattle. (pp.14–15)

No kind of critical twisting and turning can lift this tawdry material to a level where it demands attention. There are few moments in the novel which transcend this general level of ordinariness. It is all so naive – childish without being truly innocent – and yet it is supposed to be describing a man whose complexity of response must keep us engaged with the thin plot. However revealing such material may be about Malcolm Lowry in person, it fails to cross the boundaries between art and mere transcription of experience. All the greatest realist novelists, including Flaubert (whom Lowry so much admired), have been great selectors and shapers of the apparent reality they describe.

Lowry became more and more incoherent in his efforts to explain his new novel to his publishers as their unenthusiastic replies came back to chunks of the book he submitted. On Wilderness himself he argued

> He simply doesn't know what he is. He is a sort of underground man. He is also Ortega's fellow, making up his life as he goes along . . . Moreover he is disinterested in literature, uncultured, incredibly unobservant, in many respects ignorant, without faith in himself, and lacking nearly all the qualities you normally associate with a novelist . . . His very methods of writing are absurd, and he sees practically nothing at all, save through his wife's eyes . . . (*SL*, pp.331–2, *passim*)

The coolness of agent and publisher is scarcely surprising. The really significant thing is not that Lowry has tried to present a strange 'underground man', a modern anti-hero, but that he offers absolutely no rationale for *why* he seeks to do this. Nor how he proposes to make such a protagonist anything but a painful drag for the reader. Thus the whimsy and flatness of Wilderness as a centre of interest is never shown to have any purpose other than reflecting his creator. We are still supposed to sympathise with this figure, however, and to share a spiritual discovery with him at the end of the novel. Authorial assertion that 'I believe [I] can make him a very original character, both human and pathetically unhuman at once' (*idem*), leaves a huge gap between intention and execution. Dana Hilliot could be excused his callowness, not only on grounds of youth, but because he had a programme with which we could sympathise. The stature of Geoffrey Firmin and his ability to represent Everyman in a crumbling world gave him real dignity. But while he deliberately eschews dignity, Wilderness gives us no clear indication as to what his programme might be. Ostensibly it is to find Juan Cerillo. This is limited enough as an objective. In itself it may help Wilderness, but it will not do the reader much good. And even this objective is blurred by intermediate vacillations and tangents. There are other moments when Wilderness's programme actually seems to comprise discovering how beastly he can be to the vapid but long-suffering Primrose before she finally cracks under the strain. *Dark as the Grave* contains long passages which merely record the profoundly unpleasant side of Lowry's own later character. There are plenty of novels which describe unpleasant men; but there are few which apparently seek to elicit sympathy for such men because they are critically unaware of how unpleasant they are.

It would redeem matters if it could be argued that we watch the collapse and finally the redemption of a tormented soul. But the opening chapters cut us off from this idea. The first part of the novel simply presents a neurotic who could do with being shaken upside down in some infernal machine. 'Bourgeois drip' is the description of Wilderness which comes all too readily to mind.

Later there are murky impressions of a psychic disturbance of some magnitude. Wilderness suffers a curious version of the medieval deadly sin of acedia – sloth – and it is painful to watch a fellow human being who is unable to raise even a hand to help himself because of the burden he feels weighing upon him. Even here one feels a lack of clarity about the nature and origin of this burden, which was successfully evoked in Geoffrey Firmin. So, poor old Wilderness cannot get his book published; so, he is rather maladjusted; so, he is finding the booze hard to cope with on his Mexican holiday; so, the ghosts of the past will not leave him alone; so . . . ? It is not as if Wilderness is even interested in his own state in the same way that Plantagenet in *Lunar Caustic* is concerned about his. It is Wilderness or nothing, and he is simply never interesting enough to carry the burden of his own book.

Thus if its quests are two-fold, or bifurcated – that is, to find inner stasis by purging the past, and by facing the present – it fails on both counts. It is partly based upon a self-defeating irony; the past is not shown to be nearly as bad as Wilderness had built it into seeming to be, or at least time has meliorated its savageness. The Farolito is no more; 'Stanford' has become merely a fat and shifty old hen-pecked bore. And both the Wildernesses are so ordinary and so unself-aware, so coy at times, that the reader finds it hard to be deeply committed to the future well-being of their ménage – beyond feeling that Primrose may actually be worth something just a little better than all this.

The book is much more successful in those parts where the quest for Juan Cerillo is at its centre. Though he never actually appears he is able to hold our attention as Sigbjørn himself cannot. He has genuine charisma. Rogue and altruist at once, the shock of discovering he is dead is certainly the best managed thing in the entire novel. There is a justified sense of waste and desolation about the writing here which is very moving. And because Cerillo is attractive as a character, and has emotional and political integrity, so is the emotion valid through which his spirit is celebrated right at the end. It is a pity, in terms of poetic justice, that he was not killed on duty – like the bank messenger in *Under the Volcano*. His memorial as a charismatic and altruistic man is a fine and valuable one though it might have been celebrated in prose of a rather higher quality:

> It was all so different from eight years ago, and also the look of the animals, which were not shabby or starved looking but had strong well-fed looks and shining coats that came from proper feeding and care, and the fields themselves were rich. Oaxaca had become the granary of nearly all of Mexico . . .
> 'That's all the Ejidal!'
> And then a field of young, new wheat – pale green in contrast to the dark green of alfalfa – and then a field of ripening wheat dimming to gold, then quince and peach orchards, young trees, obviously planted within the last ten years and blossoming . . .
> The Banco Ejidal had become a garden.
> Then they were leaving the state of Oaxaca behind them, and behind them, too, in the dark church . . . one candle burning . . . (p.255)

The title of the novel, taken from an elegy by the seventeenth-century metaphysical poet Abraham Cowley, suggests that obsequies are to be made for Cerillo – the 'friend'. He is to be laid in his grave, metaphorically, by Wilderness as mourner. But he is also to be 'laid', as a ghost is exorcised. In the novel's last few pages both senses come close to fulfilment. Though incompletely integrated one can also see how the visits to Yautepec, to Mitla, and to Etla, provide a tonal quality which could have been worked up to serve this sense of repose even through death and mutability. But much work remained to be done on the book; most of the time we are guessing at what might have been.

Its other great limitation is that the sense of spiritual discovery which comes to the protagonist is inadequate to leave us convinced that it will have permanent value for him. Wilderness has been such a neurotic mess that one cannot trust the spirit of release of the last few pages. Perhaps this feeling is unfairly exacerbated by the knowledge of Lowry's own later career. But where an author creates fiction so close to autobiographical fact such feelings are very difficult to

resist. Both *Ultramarine* and *Dark as the Grave* pose problems of fina
resolution; in each book the hero has reached a tenuous moment o
repose, but leaves us unconvinced of its permanence. Perhaps it i
significant that of his four novels Lowry achieves real roundednes
of conclusion only in the tragic plot of *Under the Volcano*.

For the serious student of *Under the Volcano* there is every reason t
read *Dark as the Grave*; it contains succinct and germane comment o
places and events from the greater work. But it must be genuinely i
doubt whether *Dark as the Grave* would actually make much sense t
a reader whose first acquaintance with Lowry it provided. Whateve
incidentals and parcels we may salvage from it, this must be a seriou
indictment of the basic authorial assumption that autobiography ca
be transmuted into dynamic fiction without the filter of intense an
rigorous critical scrutiny. *Dark as the Grave* is a self-indulgent boo
about a self-indulgent man. Far too much of it records privat
and personal thinking in which quite inadequate efforts have bee
made to universalise and give shape and rhythm to events whic
are not intrinsically of great interest. Without such a process o
redistillation slices hacked out of a not very interesting life canno
make charismatic art.

Over the entire proceedings hangs the feeling that this is th
writing of a man who now has increasingly little to write about
The problem of the one-book author becomes even more urgen
when that author is a compulsive writer. About what else can suc
a man write except his own inability to create outside himself eithe
plot or characters which can hold the reader in the grip of genuinel
shared experiences? Sooner or later the writer who is absolutel
locked in himself is going to become simply a bore or a museum
exhibit. In the case of much of the work in *Dark as the Grave* it is
sadly, sooner.

The genesis of *October Ferry to Gabriola* bears an ominous relation
ship to all the other posthumous work. First there must be a persona
experience – preferably a voyage or quest. Copious notes will b
kept; wayside signs, unusual coincidences, and incidental trauma
will be recorded. At the end of the visit these notes will be worke
up into a short story. Very slowly this will grow towards the hybri
and indeterminate state which Lowry called 'novella'. A suspicio
develops that Lowry liked this name increasingly as the years wen
on. It seemed to console him for the halfway-house condition i
which much of his work existed. Never once does he offer a critica

definition or defence of the novella as such. By the time he was at work on *October Ferry* Lowry was desperately yawing from project to project, unable to discipline his attenuated imaginative forces. Work on the novel – which itself began as part of a short story collection – alternated with at least a dozen other projects. This is quite unlike the work method which produced *Ultramarine* and *Under the Volcano*. Bits of the first novel had themselves appeared as short stories, but there was always a guiding urge to produce one long and sustained work. And during the years of redrafting his masterpiece Lowry wrote little extraneous fiction. This implies a steady commitment to a task he absolutely believed in, and contrasts sadly with his state of mind during his later work. From about 1950 onwards publishers and agents certainly became concerned about Lowry's ability to sustain one finishable major task. In hindsight the critic can only sanction that anxiety.

Everything seemed to militate against repose and concentration. The periods of stasis at Dollarton were increasingly interspersed with trips abroad, when virtually nothing got done. There is much evidence in the last decade of Lowry's life that even his iron constitution was reaching alcoholic saturation point. Hospitalisation became more regular and more frequent; there was an increasing self-awareness that the underlying problems might be psychic rather than merely physical or social.

The technique of layering in over a thin basic story line might well encourage dispersed concentration. And one can discern, during the period when *La Mordida* and *Dark as the Grave* are both tugging for Lowry's attention and rapidly being superseded by the growth of *October Ferry*, how the close linkages between the originating real-life events made it difficult for an undisciplined mind to keep them artistically separate.

Both *Dark as the Grave* and *La Mordida* comprise episodes from the same trip to Mexico of less than six months duration. Expecting to get two full novels out of one such visit implies very limited ability to invent plots. The notebooks for the late work give away the process of creativity Lowry is using. They record everyday events, or observed phenomena which are to be deployed as motifs in the fiction. But even within one entry a curiously indeterminate mood prevails; the record oscillates between 'Malcolm said' and 'x said' – 'x' being whatever fictive name the observer bears at the time. Subjective identification with fictive personality has become dangerously intimate. Furthermore, all the later stories concern either one man alone or one man and his hyperdependent wife. There are no alternative centres of interest, no middle-ground characters of the kind provided by Hugh, Yvonne and Jacques in *Under the Volcano* With subject matter dangerously narrow, this isolationist tendency pushes the late works still further in upon themselves. Lowry was simply not interested enough in anything outside himself to feed and enrich the self-centred vision he studiously cultivated. And while the years at Dollarton were therapeutic in one way, they cut him off dangerously from intercourse with other writers, and from a consequent extension of his range or style. Both *La Mordida* and *Dark as the Grave* are fraught with the potential for failure from their inception. Malcolm and Margerie go to Mexico; Malcolm's drinking gives them a bad time – novel one. The Mexican *Migración* gives them a bad time – novel two. The supporting cast consists of what Malcolm thought, what Malcolm did not do, and very occasionally, a wild stab at what Margerie perhaps thought Malcolm was thinking.

All the universality and the human commitment of the war theme, the political theme, the Faustus theme which enriched *Under the Volcano* is absent. Far from being a failed mage as Geoffrey Firmin had been, one feels that Sigbjørn Wilderness could not pull handkerchiefs from a top hat. The Wildernesses are appallingly introverted They hardly meet anyone else, talk to strangers, go places with friends. Quite the reverse; they *refuse* invitations to accompany other peoples' trips. They would much rather hang about at the rear of second-class buses squeezing hands and indulging a private language. This is 'real' enough. There are moods and phases when we all do it. Such phases usually represent the least charismatic, the most boring and irritating stages of our lives as viewed by outsiders. An extraordinary effort of imagination is required to sharpen and direct this material into universally valid fiction. By the early 1950s Lowry is only capable of that effort in brief spasms.

This is not the end of the problem, however. Lowry's style had never been assured or consistent. Even in *Under the Volcano* there are huge sweeping perorations which are scarcely in control, but most of these are suffused with a sense of driving purpose relevant to the character conceived, and many are dramatically appropriate to the tragically failing coordination of the protagonist. There is a huge if wayward sweep to the imagination of Geoffrey Firmin. None of the later protagonists demonstrates this innate quality of mind. As Lowry's central figures become more incorrigibly middle class and intellectually unambitious, so they become duller and smaller.

Even beyond the activity of dramatic character creation *Dark as the Grave* and *October Ferry* are marred by bad writing. The problem is often signalled by lack of control and overall drive in the sentences. Once the grammatical discipline goes, the lyrical drive and the common sense go with it. The following may serve as an example:

> Yet not even the catastrophe of this, an event of the sheerest most eerie mischance, or so it seemed at the time; the house, solid, built to last forever by his great-great-grand-uncle in 1790 – two years before that amiable old pioneer (or genial old crook, who as though to establish well in advance such an arrangement need not be *une fantaésie bien Amiricaine* (*sic*) or dependent upon ultra-rapid-or-modern modes of travel, had another more lavish house in what was now Codrington, in the island of Barbados, where, in addition to a mulatto mistress, he kept a pet crocodile) took his seat in the first Canadian Parliament there at Niagara-on-the-Lake – the ancient house of Ethan's birth taking fire in the night when there was no one in it, while they were away for the weekend in Ixion, and burning to the ground for no reason anyone had been able to determine (unless, as there was certainly some cause to believe, it had been struck by lightning, an explanation almost worse than none), not even this had produced in him such a shocking reaction to the outer world of makeshift and homelessness as had now this threat of eviction from Eridanus. (*October Ferry*, pp.69–70)

In *Under the Volcano* Lowry had produced one of the longest sentences in modern English prose as the Consul copulates with the prostitute María (Chapter 12). But if that sentence is contrasted with the above unbolted and amorphous mess, a qualitative difference is clear. Firmin's sentence is a dramatic experience in itself. The forced act of coition echoes the structure of the prose, and probably occupies the same actual time to accomplish. Its divergences and tangents are all seminal to ideas which have been floated elsewhere. The sentence is broken and confused because the mind of the thinker is broken and confused. And that confusion has already encompassed our pity. There is integrity of relationship between the shape of ideas and the shape of the prose. But with this passage from *October Ferry* we have been given no supportive material to help us accept the disorganisation. It vacillates. And if Llewelyn is himself a vacillator, he is a very ordinary and unexciting one. The effort required to unpick his sentence is simply not worth making.

Those who knew him testify that these parabolic word-circuses were typical of Lowry's own speech. But unless a fictive character has been established as a legitimate creator of such parabolas they are a dubious vehicle for the communication of commonplace ideas. Such bravura writing was frequent in *Ultramarine*. There it marks deliberate experimental attempts to colour up selected moments of introspection. They are consistent to one level of Hilliot's youthful consciousness, and they are, forgivably, the work of a young and inexperienced author. Granted that the two later novels have not been finally worked over by the author, it still remains a token of muddled thought that these passages exist in the available manuscripts.

Revision for Lowry usually meant overlaying and making things more dense. One can only see the prose getting actually muddier and less coherent in later drafts. The saddest token of Lowry's own muddled mind is provided by the letters of explanation and exegesis which were supposed to defend and explain the late work to his publisher and agent. These are stumbling and incoherent. The letter to his friend David Markson (August 1951) 'explaining' *In Ballast to the White Sea* is nearly incomprehensible; it is utterly sad to compare it with the brilliant exposition of *Under the Volcano* which Lowry had written for Cape. The efforts from 1953–4 to help Erskine understand the plan of *October Ferry* are disastrously confused, and tactically fatal. Control over even the ability to tell the story of a story seems to be slipping away from Lowry.

In neither posthumous novel as we have it does one see consistent achievement with the layering-in process. Whereas in *Under the Volcano* every bird, beast and shadow genuinely enriches the centre of the work, no such controlling dynamism runs through the last novels. Their narrative shape bears no comparison with the wonderful twelve-hour, twelve-month, twelve-spoked wheel of *Under the Volcano*. *October Ferry* is broken down into 37 chapters of very unequal length – a physical shape quite unlike any other that Lowry created. This makes it difficult to judge the intended final shape of the book. It has the customary feature of scanty surface movement ramified by sweeps of retrospect. But *October Ferry* is the only Lowry novel to show much interest in the future. We can at least guess at a more integrated future for Ethan and Jacqueline than for Sigbjørn and Primrose. Wilderness is principally concerned with staving off the effects of time past during time present. The Llewellyns are all the time hoping to build for time to come. Attempts to read the book as a healthy new direction, however, grasp at tenuous straws.

Albert Erskine, the editor at Random House, expressed bewilderment and horror at what he felt were the manifest defects of *October Ferry* when he first saw material from it in the early 1950s (cf. Bowker, p.189, for instance).

The expedition which formed the germ of the story of *October Ferry* was made by the Lowrys in October 1946. The Vancouver Harbour Authority had issued yet another of its threats to develop the Dollarton area as civic amenity space, informing the squatters that they would either have to move or face bills for back taxes. The Lowrys were thus forced to seek an alternative solitude. Gabriola Island in the Gulf of Georgia seemed a viable spot. Margerie had an ex-schoolfriend who lived there and the island was still comparatively undeveloped – important for both financial and social reasons. So they set out from the mainland across to Victoria on Vancouver Island, by bus up the coast to the port of Nanaimo, and then almost on the third side of a triangle turning homeward by ferry again over to Gabriola. The journey adopted a shape capable of assuming a symbolic function, and the novel, unfinished as it may be, does have an intermittent sense of purposeful structure. There is a correlation between the geographical 'turn' towards Gabriola, and the new sense of purpose and integration in Llewelyn near the end of the book.

Nothing concrete came of the visit in terms of moving house, but within a matter of weeks it had become the matter of a short story, and then of expansion towards a novella. It began as a shared project. Margerie says '. . . we took notes, and when we returned we decided we had a short story, which we wrote together. But we decided it wasn't really first rate and it was put aside', though Day implies that some of the material used in the novel existed before the Gabriola visit (Day, p.303). It is uncertain at what precise stage the actual 'Gabriola' material (the eviction theme) and the loss of the shack (the 'conflagration' theme) became assimilated. By November 1950 a version of the story had been sent to Hal Matson – 'a story which you've had before, but which was no damned good. This we decided we couldn't collaborate on so I have completely rewritten it by myself and finally I'm extremely pleased with it . . .' (*SL*, p.216).

From about this time the story which had been simmering in the background grew into an all-embracing project. The letter to Matson promises *October Ferry* should be 'in the post in a week'. Erskine hears, in June 1951, that 'scares of eviction come and go, and it is a situation of some universal significance I have always meant to develop in the novel'. The plot of *October Ferry*, Lowry complains, 'gets into all the short stories too'. A further letter to Matson in October 1951 lists the project as 'another novella . . . (which) . . . I've completely redrafted and rewritten, and it deals with the theme of eviction, which is related to man's dispossession, but this theme is universalised'. At a tangent Lowry also discussed at about this time with David Markson the subsidiary theme of the boy sentenced to hang for a rape he did not commit. The eviction theme was kept alive by subsequent scares: in May 1952 a letter to Erskine describes evacuation plans should Dollarton become uninhabitable.

From early 1953 the tempo increases. *October Ferry* has now ousted *Dark as the Grave* and *La Mordida* as 'the current and besetting problem'. Lowry expresses great excitement at the extent to which 'for months' it has been taking him over – 'it grew almost to a novel on its own' – (*SL*, p.328). The new work had to be prevented from 'greedily gulping' material which rightly belongs to *Eridanus*. In other words, a welter of heterogeneous material is yoking itself by violence to whichever manuscript he happens to set out on that day or that week. Later in the same year he declares that his new favourite project has cost him more pains even than *Under the Volcano* and it has now become a not-so-short novel. An inkling of Erksine's tepid response has dawned on Lowry by now, and the defensive exegeses become more and more frenetic. He promises that the new novel is going to be a 'psychological triumph of the first order', but, alas, this is a reference to Lowry's own state of mind in writing it, not to the accomplishment within the work. And then the cat is really let out of the bag:

> . . . it possesses perhaps not one single conventional virtue of the normal story – its character drawing is virtually non-existent, symbols are pointed at blatantly instead of being . . . subsumed . . . it is repetitious . . . (*SL*, p.339)

Then, the most extraordinary confession of all — it is all done on purpose! He sounds like a man who has lost all grasp upon the realities of publishing viable fiction.

November 1953 finds Lowry attempting to allay Erskine's scepticism with a schematic exegesis of *October Ferry*, but it is difficult to believe Lowry was sober when he wrote it; '. . . I will expound thus far the magic of Dr. Lowry's dialectical-Hegelian-spiritualism-Cabbalistic-Swedenborgian-conservative-Christian-anarchism for ailing paranoiacs' (*SL*, p.346).

Early in 1954 Random House terminated Lowry's running contract. He had offered them very little which was saleable and completed. The preoccupation with dashing from project to project offered Erskine no assurance that he would ever see work for his cash. At least half a dozen short stories were being carried forward at the same time, and their relationship to each other (and to *October Ferry*) was still not fixed. There is a strong implication that for a long time *October Ferry* was intended as the penultimate story in the collection which became *Hear Us O Lord* (*SL*, p.356), and this must have compounded the confusion at Random House — especially as Lowry moots cutting two hundred pages from the current five hundred at which the manuscript stands. And Lowry is also trying to prise a lump off it to be published as a short story in its own right. (This eventually appeared in *Show* magazine in 1964 as 'The Element Follows You Around Sir'). The current favourite brainchild receives typical defence; it will not admit of stock responses; the reader needs to be already sold on the result before he begins the process of reading; it does not aim to be a good book.

When the Lowrys finally left Canada *October Ferry* went with them. We hear from Malcolm in hospital late in 1955 that the last eighteen months have been barren. The doctor has forbidden him to write on the Gabriola theme, though by December the next year he is 'working like absolute sin' on it (*SL*, p.393), and Day avers that it was preoccupying him just before his death in June 1957.

Thus, on and off, it had been every bit as long in gestation as *Under the Volcano*. But *October Ferry* had not been worked upon with the same creative concentration. Strands of narrative and symbols lack a fiery coherence. Ten years of work have produced an unfinished book which is still extremely tentative.

For all that, it is a more interesting work than *Dark as the Grave*. The universal significance of the theme of eviction does show itself, albeit shadowly, and the minor motifs hint how Ethan Llewellyn could have become a type of human dispossession. While Victoria Island offers none of the startling local colour which enlivens *Under the Volcano* it is sensitively felt, and evoked with skill. Part of the problem in the book centres in the wife, Jacqueline. Even more than Primrose Wilderness she is a meek and docile fetcher and carrier of baggage and bits of ideas.

The novel tries to bind together a number of preoccupations which have scarred the life of its hero. These may be designated as follows:

(a) eviction from home
(b) professional guilt
(c) conscience over failures of civic responsibility
(d) anger over civilisation's sell-out of individual sensibility
(e) the problems of allowing pity to dominate pragmatism
(f) pathological shyness
(g) the relationship between reality and occult forces,
      particularly supranormal coincidence.

There is plenty here to work on. The struggle was to make the various strands cohere. Dashing off into short stories and other abortive projects did not help. Equally obstructive was the half-hearted attempt to make Ethan Llewellyn into yet another alcohol-fixated hero. This motif is never rigorously pursued; with all his other hang-ups did Llewellyn *need* a drink problem too? Though several of its scenes are set in beer halls, drink is no longer central to the matter of action and conscience in *October Ferry*. It is as though Lowry has labelled himself a writer who specialises in alcoholics, and he cannot conceive of a character who does not have the problem.

At least we are free of the feeling Wilderness gave us, that a good day's hard work might sort him out. Ethan's struggle to reconcile himself to abdication from his profession as lawyer is a legitimate interest.

The theme of eviction is familiar from *Under the Volcano*. Lowry's own evictions from Mexico, and the threatened one from Dollarton, have sharpened this and it becomes the major narrative motif in *October Ferry*. The ostensible purpose of the bus ride which occupies the one day of time present is to seek an alternative home. Most of the parabolas of thought which arc outwards into time past draw upon the same theme. On a level near the narrative surface there is some good rousing writing about conservative and unimaginative Authority as it interferes with individual privacy. The new home is a token of a new start, and of a new integration and moral centre for Ethan. Other themes are pencilled in to corroborate this, though few are more than light sketches. The Wandering Jew, Parsifal, Tristan all make intermittent chords in the background of the book, and might, with further work, have been intensified and made more coherent.

Lowry also makes use of the cinema – as he had done in *Under the Volcano*; voices from the screen boom things like 'A fugitive and a wanderer shalt thou be in the earth' at the emotionally displaced Llewellyns, and titles like Griffith's 'Isn't Life Wonderful?' recur to add an ironic undertow to the events surrounding them. The notion of displacement is further underlined by a comic lack of certainty about Ethan's national identity. A Canadian, brought up in England, and now under threat of dispossession back in his native land, he is also noticeably like all the other Lowry heroes in being alienated from even tenuous ties with his immediate family. Jacqueline is also the child of a highly contentious parentage. Hence, presumably, the epigraph from *Troilus and Criseyde* (Book 1, 416–18) which prefaces the book:

Al stereless with-inne a boot am I
A-mid the see, by-twixen windes two,
That in contrarie standen ever-mo.

Ethan has always been homeless, or cut off from domestic repose. Fire pursues him with tragi-comic intensity; merely looking at a picture of a possible future domicile is enough to bring about spontaneous combustion to the premises. This also brings in the motif of the spooky coincidences which dog him. This side of the book is extended by the personality and influence of Jacqueline's father, The McCandless, who is a white magician. All these, of course, are preoccupations close to Lowry himself.

Ethan has a persecution complex. His psychic instability is deepened by guilt. He has been an excellent defence lawyer, with a national reputation. But now he is in retirement, because he defended a prisoner, believing in his innocence, who subsequently turned out to be guilty. Now fingers of remorse poke at Ethan since,

currently, a sixteen year old is likely to suffer the death penalty for
a rape he did not commit. Should Ethan return to the bar to defend
him? This is constantly cross-cut with the guilt he feels about Peter
Cordwainer, who had been an undergraduate friend of Ethan. He
committed suicide, after confessing his intention to Llewellyn, who
did nothing to stop him. So a very private and a very public civic
responsibility intermingle. Cordwainer's face had been featured in
a picture advertising a brand of soup, and this advertisement haunts
Ethan, recurring at alarming moments from hoardings along the road
as the bus progresses. This montage technique is familiar from *Under
the Volcano* – though it played little part in *Dark as the Grave* – and it
offers a handy way of drawing in the guilt theme.

Ethan is also bothered about his status and responsibility *vis-à-vis*
officialdom. It is difficult sometimes to reconcile his hypersensitive
reticence with what must have been the exigencies of his life as
a lawyer. He cowers in corners like a guilty schoolboy. But it
helps along some of the book's most nicely observed whimsy
in the drinking-hall scenes. The eminent defence council is in
mortal terror of discovery in breach of Vancouver's lunatic and
insensitive licensing laws. There is real verve in the writing of these
episodes, and a balanced ability by Lowry equally to laugh at and
to sympathise with his hero. Such brushes with officialdom readily
spill over onto a sense of responsibility to defend the innocent earth
itself against vandalism in the guise of City Council development
policy. In snatches this theme has rhetorical power, and Lowry
provokes the belief that civilisation quickly comes to mean nothing
more than the organisation of the lowest common denominator of
ignorance and prejudice into a vehicle of self-satisfied destruction.
'All the mountain howitzers, skoda guns, spavined horses and mules
available to the moral forces of municipal Canadian non-judicial
opinion', as he puts it in Chapter 7.

The book is on strong ground here, but its problem is to keep
the Llewellyns themselves lively enough to sustain and warrant
the indignation expressed. They lapse at times merely into an
incorrigibly middle-class desire to preserve a status quo for their
own benefit. Whether revision could have purged the novel of these
blemishes must remain matter for conjecture. So long as finding a
new home is integrated as a motif with achieving spiritual purgation
one can believe in the book. For long passages it is unable to sustain
this – the new house becomes a bourgeois dream in its own right.

Pity and pragmatism fight a battle in Ethan Llewellyn. When pity wins he seems a fine-natured man; but there are moments when self-pity supervenes. Part of the problem lies in Jacqueline. She is not strong enough as a character to have any battle taking place in her own consciousness; she seems merely an echo of Ethan rather than a dramatic complement to him. In describing her background Lowry tried almost too hard to elicit pity for her. It comes as a real and pleasant surprise in Chapter 26 when for once Jacqueline fights back. One would have wished further revisions to the novel to strengthen her still further.

The problem of controlling and channelling the emotion of pity has its centre in Ethan's mistaken defence of a guilty man. It is not quite clear what made Lowry fix on the law as a vocation for his hero, and the ground he treads with Ethan's professional life is not always sure. Would so eminent a defence council suddenly take fright in this way? Guilt over action he *did* take in this case spills over onto action he *did not* take in the case of Cordwainer. We are given the impression that Ethan is assuming too much guilt for what happened to Cordwainer. But perhaps it is better to care too much than not to care enough. He certainly cares, too, about the unfortunate teenager being held in jail in Vancouver, accused falsely of a rape. Llewellyn is the only Lowry protagonist except Geoffrey Firmin to care what happens to other people, and with all his weaknesses it makes him a refreshing change.

The attempt is also made to create a character whose public reticence and uncertainty are linked to his private phobias. Again there are moments when this works very well and creates wry humour, as Lowry makes us laugh at his hypersensitive protagonist. In Chapter 10 Ethan is foolishly drawn to interpolate himself onto the conversation of some schoolchildren who have joined the bus. The quality of the embarrassment that everyone feels – reader, children, Jacqueline, Ethan himself – is nicely captured. Poor Ethan realises that he is getting nowhere, and is compounding his error with every interjection, yet cannot stop himself. This rings very true to the minor absurdities which so often overtake casual acts of outgoingness. It helps us to see inside this strange, lonely, but basically benevolent man.

Many of the moments of such comedy in *October Ferry* are well managed. Their presence saves the novel from the morbidity which blemished *Dark as the Grave*. The theme of Ethan's shyness elicits many of these moments. So does the sense of being hag-ridden by malevolent circumstance. Chapter 18 – 'The Element Follows You Around Sir' – is full of these half-whimsical, half-diabolical occurrences. All are very close to what Lowry claimed had been the truth of his stay at Niagara-on-the-Lake, after his shack had burned down.

Such visitations are still far short of the cosmic forces which had hounded Geoffrey Firmin, but they accumulate to make us feel Ethan is a man unjustly 'fingered' by some malevolent higher Authority. The book moves us slowly towards seeing him purged of his visitations. The closer the journey gets to Gabriola, the more he recovers. In Nanaimo he meets an old client whom he had successfully defended, and who still remembers him with passionate gratitude. Not only does this man make us see a fresh side to Ethan – one which his own reticence had not brought to light; it also cancels any doubts we had about his defence of a guilty client. It is one of a number of small revelations which accumulate in the last third of the novel to create a sense of new hope and regeneration. We also see that Ethan is his own worst enemy, a man well worth redeeming.

The closing sections of *October Ferry* are given a special tone and quality by two other motifs. Despite his neurotic urgency to get to Gabriola before nightfall Ethan manages genuine sympathy and altruism when the ferry has to turn back for a sick passenger. Much more than the physical help he offers, his spiritual willingness to be outgoing towards others suggests that he may be on the road to recovery from the self-centred and introspective habits of thought which have blighted him. And his strange and haunting encounter with the priest hints at a new flowing of the waters of the spirit.

There is an immediate reward; only by putting back to Nanaimo does the boat manage to collect the evening papers containing the announcement that the Llewellyns' home is to be reprieved after all. In one sense, then, the entire journey has been unnecessary. Yet in making it Ethan has come a long way towards spiritual regeneration. The tone of the writing reinforces this feeling. Only 'The Forest Path to the Spring' matches the best of the later chapters of *October Ferry* for a sense of lyrical reconciliation:

> The island lay before them in the last of the sunset light, a
> long dark shape, spiked with pines against the fading sky. There

was no splendor of gold and scarlet maples, it was a splendor of blackness, of darkness. And as they approached, there seemed no beach . . . The wind blew sharp and salt and cold . . .

Abruptly the little ferry rounded the jutting headland: at the same moment there burst forth a shattering din . . . It was the ferry, blasting on its siren with a deep, protracted chord of mournful triumph. In the sky some stars came out . . .

And now through the twilight as the echoes died away Jacqueline and Ethan distinguished the outlines of a sheltered valley that sloped down to a silent, calm harbor. Deep in the dark forest behind was the glow of a fire . . . someone was burning tree stumps to clear his land. The sound of lowing cattle was borne to them and they could see a lantern swinging along close to the ground. A voice called out, clear, across the water. And now they saw the dock, with silhouetted figures moving against a few lights that gleamed in the dusk . . . (pp.332–33)

This manifests a kind of imagination new to Lowry. After all, the real-life trip to Gabriola produced no solutions or epiphanies. The end of *October Ferry* represents one of the few occasions when Lowry goes creatively beyond himself into an optimistic world. He postulates a hero moving upwards rather than plunging downwards like Geoffrey Firmin. There is quality and control in the writing itself; it seems assured and lyrical. At first Gabriola stands dark, inscrutable, potentially hostile or rejective. So it had been with life itself earlier in the day. There is a gradual transformation. Dimly it can be discerned that the island *does* offer a harbour. It is peopled. The element of fire has been subdued here; it is useful, not destructive. The dark is broken by human voices.

There the novel ends on a lyrical up-beat. *Dark as the Grave* attempts a similar surge of the spirit, but the effort is forced and perfunctory in comparison. Llewellyn *deserves* to feel better; Wilderness has never earned a similar release.

It remains a critical question whether the correlatives of fear and spiritual torment are always adequately presented and sustained in *October Ferry*. They are by no means uniformly layered in, nor coherently spread through the book. The character of Jacqueline's father – The McCandless – is disappointingly underdeveloped. He hints at being one of Lowry's richest comic creations. Some of the themes – the parallels with Parsifal particularly – have scarcely begun to assume coherent and creative shape. The son, Tommy, appears to be an original tactical error which Lowry never corrected. Having created the Llewellyns as the only couple in his fiction to have a child, Lowry does absolutely nothing with him. But the very idea shows him trying to break new ground.

There remains, too, the problem of plot-movement, a problem symptomatic of so much of Lowry's fiction. The novel's 'narrative and dramatic interest', to use Erskine's phrase, is very thin on the surface of the book. Yet there is promise of new directions being explored in *October Ferry*. The theme of the tortured drunken writer was so obviously played out that Lowry *had to* find new directions for his compulsive and introspective writing. For all its flaws and inconsistencies *October Ferry* is a brave attempt to strike out in a new direction.

Notes

1. Douglas Day, *Malcolm Lowry: A Biography* (London: Oxford University Press, 1973).
2. Gordon Bowker, *Malcolm Lowry Remembered* (London: Ariel Books, 1985).
3. Harvey Breit and Margerie Bonner Lowry (eds.), *The Selected Letters of Malcolm Lowry* (London: Jonathan Cape, 1967).

These are referred to in the text as 'Day'; 'Bowker'; '*SL*', respectively.

4. This novella was first published in *The Paris Review*, VIII, 29 (Winter–Spring, 1963), pp.12–72. Then (London: Jonathan Cape) 1968. Then with *Hear Us O Lord* by Penguin Books, Harmondsworth, 1979. All quotations in this book are taken from the latter edition.
5. T. Bareham, 'The Englishness of Malcolm Lowry', *Journal of Commonwealth Literature*, December 1976, Vol.XI, No.2, pp.134–49.
6. Russell Lowry has written twice about his younger brother's early years:
(a) in Anne Smith (ed.), *The Art of Malcolm Lowry* (London: Vision Press Ltd., 1978)
(b) in Bowker (see note 2 above).
7. *SL*, p.149.
8. Bowker has several accounts of the nature and quantity of Lowry's drinking.
9. Bowker, pp.46–9.
10. Bowker, *passim*.
11. Two Lowry short stories are based upon these months of fraught marriage:
(a) 'In Le Havre', *Life and Letters*, X, 55 (July 1934), pp.642–66
(b) 'Hotel Room in Chartres', *Story*, V, 26 (September 1934), pp.53–8.
12. Richard K. Cross, *Malcolm Lowry: A Preface to his Fiction* (London: University of Chicago Press, 1980, p.115).
13. In an interview with Gordon Bowker entitled 'The Lighthouse Invites The Storm'; BBC, 1984.
14. Gerald Noxon, 'Malcolm Lowry: 1930', *Prairie Schooner* XXXVII, 4 (Winter 1963–4), pp.315–20.
15. Lowry's attitude to Mexico should be contrasted with that of

Graham Greene, Aldous Huxley, Evelyn Waugh and D.H. Lawrence, who all use Mexico for the *mise-en-scène* of some of their writing in the 1920s and 1930s.

16. Earle Birney, with the assistance of Margerie Lowry (ed.), *Selected Poems of Malcolm Lowry* (San Francisco: City Lights Books, 1962).

17. This is admirably represented in Ackerley and Clipper's *Companion* (see Bibliography).

18. Arthur Osborne Lowry died early in 1945.

19. Published 1945.

20. *The Voyage That Never Ends* was the trilogy planned to bring together *Under the Volcano* (Inferno); *Lunar Caustic* (Purgatorio); *In Ballast to the White Sea* (Paradiso). Cf. *SL*, pp.63, 113, 245, 255 for descriptions.

Bibliography

LOWRY'S MAJOR FICTION

First American and first English editions are described where these differ. Page references throughout this volume are from the first English edition, unless otherwise stated.

Ultramarine (London: Jonathan Cape, 1933; new and revised edition, 1963). Reference in this book is to the Penguin Books edition (Harmondsworth, 1974).

Under the Volcano (London: Jonathan Cape, 1947; New York: Reynall and Hitchcock, 1947). Reference in this book is to the paperback edition (Harmondsworth: Penguin Books, 1963).

Hear Us O Lord from Heaven Thy Dwelling Place (Philadelphia: Lippincott, 1961; London: Jonathan Cape,1962). Subsequently issued along with *Lunar Caustic* (see below) (Harmondsworth: Penguin Books,1979).Reference in this book is to this edition, designated PMC (Penguin Modern Classics).

Lunar Caustic first appeared in *The Paris Review*, VIII (Winter–Spring 1963, pp. 12–72), edited by Earle Birney and Margerie Lowry, with a Preface by Conrad Knickerbocker. Then (London:Jonathan Cape) 1968.

Dark as the Grave Wherein My Friend is Laid (New York: New American Library,1968; London:Jonathan Cape, 1969).

October Ferry to Gabriola (New York:World,1970; London: Jonathan Cape, 1971).

*Malcolm Lowry:Psalms and Songs.*Edited by Margerie Lowry (New York: New American Library,1975). This last title contains pieces about Lowry as well as material by him. Since the scope of my study is intended to cover the novels and the *interrelated* short stories, I have not considered it for critical commentary here.

A SHORT LIST OF BOOKS ABOUT LOWRY

Further works of criticism and background are cross referred from the text to the Notes.

Ackerley, Chris, and Clipper, Lawrence J., *A Companion to Under the Volcano* (Vancouver: University of British Columbia Press, 1984).

Bradbrook, M.C., *Malcolm Lowry: His Art and Early Life* (London: Cambridge University Press, 1974).

Costa, Richard Hauer, *Malcolm Lowry* (New York: Twayne Books, 1972).

Dodson, Daniel B., *Malcolm Lowry* (London: Columbia University Press, 1970).

Epstein, Perle, *The Private Labyrinth of Malcolm Lowry* (New York: Holt, Rinehart, 1969).

Markson, David, *Malcolm Lowry's 'Volcano': Myth, Symbol, Meaning* (New York: Times Books, 1978).

New, William H., *Malcolm Lowry: A Reference Guide* (London: Oxford University Press, 1978).

Index